Creating a
Natural Garden

Creating a Natural Garden

Michael Jefferson-Brown

WARD LOCK

First published in Great Britain in 1991
by Ward Lock Limited, Villiers House,
41/47 Strand, London WC2N 5JE, England
A Cassell Imprint
© Ward Lock Ltd

Text filmset in Formby
by Chapterhouse
Printed and bound in Portugal
by Resopal

British Library Cataloguing in Publication Data
Jefferson-Brown, Michael *1930–*
   Creating a natural garden.
   1. Gardening
   I. Title   II. Series
   635

   ISBN 0–7063–6979–3

CONTENTS

PREFACE

'The Natural Garden' may be thought a contradiction in terms. A garden is obviously unnatural, and nature would soon transform it if the gardener was not around to monitor its 'naturalness'.

The word 'natural' in the title of this book is taken to have two meanings. The first is the design idea of the garden as a community of plants which, by their casual association, lend emphasis to each other's character. This is the opposite of the rigidly formal garden where plants are marshalled in rows and blocks, and the hand of the gardener is evident in the position of almost every leaf and petal.

The second sense in which the descriptive word 'natural' is used applies to the practical management of the garden. Here the suggestion is that plants should be chosen for their ability to manage their own affairs, that they are left alone, and that the gardener's role is merely to accentuate the best of the natural features of the garden and the ways of nature. Contours of the ground want to be exploited rather than eliminated. The existence of wet areas can be welcomed for the opportunity to grow a range of plants which rely on wet conditions. Necessary digging is not frowned on but nature's way of dropping annual layers of dead leaves as a topping-up mulch is noted and the example followed by using composted and other natural materials in a regular mulching campaign which will look after the structure and mineral health of the soil and encourage all the beneficial life within it.

The extreme position of not allowing any manufactured chemicals as food or sprays is not taken, but again we hope to be on the side of the angels and encourage nature's own curbs on the ills that can afflict the garden. Where an early dose of spray can prevent an epidemic it is recommended – one bucket of water could stop a forest fire at the onset. However the garden is looked upon as a home of plants, birds, insects and animals, apart from the mortgage payers.

In these senses the natural garden is both a more exciting adventure than the formal one and, with a little forethought, can be maintained to look well at all times with greater ease and less expense of money and labour than the plots where bedding-out and regimentation rules. Life can be easier for the gardener because the degree of physical effort – of regular work – can be tailored to your wishes. Bedding work has to be done at certain periods. It means clearing up after the show, and organizing the next pageant. The natural garden will be an evolving and growing thing; it certainly does not involve the scene shifting, stage clearing, plant marshalling, and regular cultivations of the formal schemes.

There is enough bustle and formality in our workaday lives. Let us enjoy the garden as a natural haven where we can relax and recharge our batteries.

M.J-B.

CHAPTER 1

THE TRADITION

Gardens are subject to fashion. In Britain and elsewhere there have been alternating swings from formal to much more relaxed and nature-inspired designs. Historical evidence is mainly drawn from the records of stately homes and the monied classes. Cottagers and artisans were presumably less subject to the vagaries of fashion, being more concerned with growing something useful for the pot.

THE LARGE GARDENS

The writings of Francis Bacon (1561–1626) include descriptions of gardens with a 'natural wilderness', a somewhat tamed and managed wild area of plants, similar to the vision of William Robinson at the beginning of the twentieth century.

   The landscape garden, known on the continent as the 'jardin anglais', traces its origin back before its most famous practitioner, 'Capability' Brown (1715–1783). The poet Pope (1688–1744) had a garden in Twickenham, UK, of relatively modest dimensions but planted in such a way as to deceive visitors into thinking it was much larger; plantings disguised the limits of the rectangular form. The descriptions and sketches as shown in Fig. 1 suggest that it approached close to modern conceptions of a garden, a balance between some necessary formality and more natural effects. The kitchen garden was excluded from the main garden and the greenhouse and vineyard were carefully shielded from direct view. Pope was a friend of William Kent (1684–1748) and must have had some effect on the taste of this painter-cum-garden designer.

   'Capability' Brown enjoyed huge public acclaim. He is remembered as the most influential of landscape gardeners, putting into effect the ideas of Kent and others. He swept away hundreds of more or less formal gardens to produce idealized landscapes with lakes, woods, copses and undulating land that allowed wide vistas from the houses, vistas that might have needed the removal of a village or two. His most energetic period was from 1751, when he moved to London, until his death in 1783. He would arrive at a garden and, having thoroughly examined it, produce a plan to be followed by teams of

Opposite: A wooden bridge leads over a small stream. Plants are naturalized in a happy community that is a mix between a cottage and a wild garden.

Rock, water and foliage plants in a happy natural association. The strata of the rocks have been carefully noted before laying. Large-leaved *Gunnera manicata* contrasts with the sword-like foliage of the iris at the rear and the colourful variegated grass.

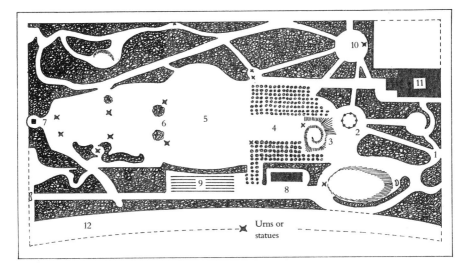

Fig. 1 Plan of the poet Pope's garden, Twickenham, 1744, drawn by his gardener John Searle. 1. The entrance from the grotto. 2. The shell temple. 3. The large mount. 4. The grove. 5. The bowling green. 6. Two small mounts. 7. Obelisk to his mother's memory. 8. The stove. 9. The vineyard. 10. The orangery. 11. The garden house. 12. The kitchen garden.

subcontractors. However, without belittling his work, it is probably fair to say that his vision was not original. Kent's idea of the ha-ha, the wide concealed ditch, was much used to keep farm animals away from the ground around the house.

THE VICTORIAN AGE

The busy Victorian age saw a huge influx of plants from all parts of the world. New technology made the culture of some more exotic ones possible under glass. Man was master of Nature and in the garden this resulted in a formality that ended in many plants growing in ranks and beds precisely regimented. Shrubs and trees were clipped into exact shapes, geometrical or fanciful representations of animals and other objects.

The inevitable reaction to this formality was led by William Robinson, a horticultural writer of immense energy and forthright views. His book *The English Flower Garden* published in 1883 proved very popular in Britain and other countries. He expounded on the open natural style that he had been advocating for many years in his weekly journal *The Garden* and other periodicals. Robinson was catering for a new gardening public, the owners of the new houses being built in the expanding towns of the Victorian age. He carried in his mind a picture of an ideal English cottage garden with its emphasis on the interest of plants; walls festooned with climbers, beds crowded with hardy plants and shrubs, and grass with sweeps of natural wild flowers.

Miss Gertrude Jekyll was a trained artist and had a good eye for colour and composition. She worked in a similar manner to Robinson's but was very much her own woman, with carefully thought out planting associations and designs. Her house, Munstead Wood, was designed by the architect Sir Edwin Landseer Lutyens and she worked in happy professional association with him for many years. Her ideas about the marriage of garden to the necessarily geometrical shape of the house continue to bear fruit today.

ROCK GARDENS

One of the twentieth century's contributions to gardening was the rock garden and the cultivation of alpine plants. The movement had its own gurus, foremost of whom was Reginald Farrer, a complex character who lived close to the limestone range at Ingleborough in north-west Yorkshire where genuine native alpines grew. Farrer laid down the ground rules for the building of rock gardens and the cultivation of many plants, always encouraging readers to learn from nature (Fig. 2).

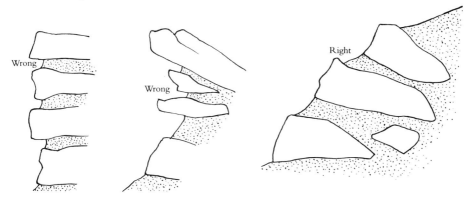

Fig. 2 Diagram from Reginald Farrer's *The English Rock Garden*, 1919.

Almost every well-known garden had to have its rock garden – some really prodigious. Sometimes the result was very contrived and even ridiculous but often a rocky naturalness was achieved. The passage of two world wars altered the economic climate and the expense of building large rock gardens became prohibitive. The rock garden was scaled down to modest proportions. It had long been realized that alpine plants could be grown happily without a rock garden. Plants were more often grown in rock beds or in containers like old troughs or sinks. Now this is almost standard practice amongst the many alpine enthusiasts, but some effort is still made to achieve a natural effect.

CHAPTER 2

TODAY'S ATTITUDES AND GARDENS

SPACE AND FASHION

Most gardens today are of modest size. Land is expensive and labour perhaps even more so. Better to manage a small plot well than be slave to what may be the delusions of grandeur. In addition, the other side of the equation is that most of us have more leisure time and greater affluence than in times past. Technology too may be put in the scales against the expense of labour and land.

What is certainly true is that the gardener at the end of the twentieth century has a greater range of plants to choose from than ever before. Species have been brought from every part of the world and breeders have busied themselves producing a wide range of new plants, most of which are easier to grow than the wildlings. In the restricted space of a garden, you can afford to be highly selective. Choices may be governed by many factors, but it is unlikely that any plant will gain easy admittance unless it has credentials to suggest it is not only beautiful in bloom but that it also has attractive foliage and form, together with exemplary habits.

Fashion can be a matter of severe practicability. The smaller cultivar gains points over the older larger one as it seems more in scale with the surroundings, and a larger variety of plants can be grown per square yard. Attempts at old-fashioned bedding – masses of colour from serried blocks of plants – are not going to be easy to manage successfully in small spaces, apart from being very expensive. The most extrovert colours may be allowed in small measure, but it is likely that the less ostentatious shades are going to marry in with the general effect far more pleasingly.

DESIGN CONSIDERATIONS

The aim may well be to achieve the maximum feeling of space, which will be easier to produce by arranging the design along natural lines rather than more formally. In practical terms this may mean putting into effect some of the following:

1. Masking, either partially or completely, the artificial boundary markers, such as walls and fences.
2. Trying to create false perspectives to suggest distances are greater than they actually are. Tapering lawns and paths away from the house will do this. So, too,

will pergolas that become just a little narrower the further away they go.

3. Creating interest by the curving lines of a path or border edge. A path may lead behind a tree or shrub to suggest further extensions. The rise and fall of ground can intrigue and deceive. A far shaded area of dark blue-green bushes can accentuate the feeling of depth.

4. Arranging plant associations that by contrast of form, colour and/or habit enhance the character of each other.

5. Planting so that there is a sense of belonging, of bulbs, herbaceous plants, shrubs, and trees living in community.

6. If possible including the sky in the design by using columnar trees to create vertical lines, and weeping species to 'pull' the sky down visually.

7. Water, whether still or moving, adds a naturally pleasing feature. There is always a touch of mystery about water: the brooding stillness of a mirror-calm pool, the eye-catching excitement where water falls over rocks or issues from a fountain.

8. Water, trees, shrubs, and the choice of plants can do a lot to attract and to help wild life. Alongside the plants, the garden becomes a thriving community of insects and animals like hedgehogs, birds, fish, frogs, newts and others sharing it with you.

9. The garden is planted with winter as fully in mind as the warmer seasons. Winter is long, summer often too short. When deciduous plants drop their leaves and herbaceous ones die down to ground level the garden still needs enough life to look interesting and beautiful. One good winter-flowering shrub or tree is worth ten of their summer-blooming relatives. Just one or two planted in prime positions can do much to banish the threatening gloom of winter (Fig. 3).

NATURAL GARDENING

There are various aspects to the movement towards natural gardening, including the design considerations which have been briefly touched upon. Also important is the planning of the garden to allow the planted community to grow

Opposite
Fig. 3: Garden design: 1. Patio. 2. Grass. 3. Mixed beds. 4. Bog and pool margin plants. 5. Witch hazel. 6. *Viburnum* 'Dawn'. 7. Dwarf conifers. 8. Fastigiate of other specimen tree or shrub. 9. Heathers, dwarf conifers and small plants. 10. Flowering cherry, apple or something similar. 11. Conifers or other evergreens. 12. Large deciduous tree. 13. Compost making area. 14. Herbaceous plants and shrubs area. 15. Wild garden. 16. Pool. 17. Rock garden/bed. 18. Scree. 19 and 20. Path, paved/gravel/shredded bark/cut grass.

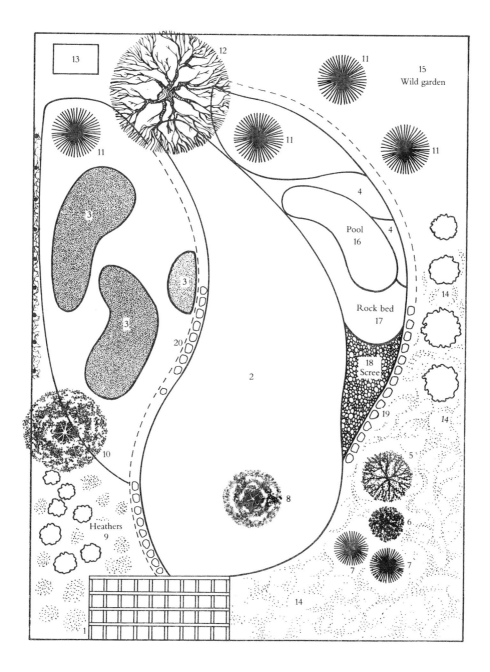

Rock garden plants grown as if on a scree with a layer of granite chippings acting as a mulch that keeps roots cool, keeps leaves dry, allows rain through and helps to conserve moisture.

Moist spots are loved by colonizing candelabra primulas like these salmon coloured *P. bulleyana* and pinky red *P. pulverulenta*. They can reach 60 cm (2 ft) or more. Flowers are about 2 cm (¾ in) in diameter.

and flourish with the minimum of digging, pruning, and replanting. There has long been a 'no digging' school of thought, and its thinking helps to underpin this aspect. Followers of no digging believe that a regular regime of topdressing imitates nature and encourages the action of worms and other soil organisms that keep the soil healthy and obviate the need to dig. This does not mean there is nothing to do. In fact, the impression of naturalness may hide a significant amount of planning and gentle maintenance, because unless the gardener exerts a positive influence all is likely to end as scrub, ground elder, bindweed, and a petition from the surrounding neighbours to do something about a threat to property values!

Most plants do best when left alone to get on with their own affairs, with the gardener only providing protection from the incursions of over exuberant neighbours and invading weeds. Hellebores hate disturbance and will do better each successive year with just enough care from you to remove dead leaves, ensure there are not too many slugs, and perhaps provide a topdressing of well rotted compost to feed the plants, stifle weed seed, and keep roots reasonably moist and cool. Michaelmas daisies and some other strong-growing herbaceous plants need more care. New pieces are detached from the outside of the clumps, planted in a fresh place in the early spring, and the older parts of the original clump discarded. If you plan to avoid such work, then your choice of plants should be restricted to those that can be left to their own devices.

The completely wild garden, an ecological unit of native plants and other wild life, is the extreme example of the trend towards natural gardening. It should be said at the outset that to start and maintain such a garden is by no means as easy as it may seem at first sight. It is merely another form of gardening and initially requires as much or more work as the traditional borders for it to be successful. A pasture or meadow full of wild flowers is delightful and it can be created even on a fairly small scale, but careful management is needed to imitate the effects of grazing farm animals or the taking of hay, and so keep the coarser grasses and weeds in check.

CONSERVATION

The wholesale destruction of plant wild life that has followed an expanded and technologically more efficient agriculture, is now being halted. Unhappily, much has been irrevocably lost; species have disappeared and others have been eradicated from former stations so that once fairly widespread kinds are now rare. The extensive use of weedkillers, first adopted by farmers and later by local authorities, often reduced the plant populations of hedgerows and verges to a few strong species. Hedgerows are often the last refuge of many species in areas where farms and building have taken over every other natural habitat.

However, more enlightened policies are now prevailing, and there is evidence of some recovery on the part of some species. It is unlawful to remove plants from the wild without the landowner's permission and there is a list of fully protected species which no one may molest in any way.

By growing some wild plants, not only is the interest of the garden increased but also the genetic pool of the wild population. There are many firms offering nursery-raised plants or seed of native plants.

HOUSE AND GARDEN

The house dominates the smaller plot but that need not stop a more natural approach to garden design. As the garden is viewed from the house, most should be made of the space and as much as possible planted to disguise intruding fences, walls or other buildings. The house may be integrated in the design by having its walls clothed with climbing and scrambling plants and by having shrubs and other plants growing around the bases of the walls to soften the outlines. With most houses the addition of plants is a visual improvement and gives a feeling of established permanence. A mature garden with a natural feeling will enhance the value of the property.

There is a wealth of shrubs and climbers that will enjoy the warmth and support of a wall. They can make a positive contribution by keeping the house warmer and protecting the walls from weathering. Such planting will encourage many birds to come closer to the house. The only major difficulty is that a narrow strip of ground by the walls can be very dry indeed, and any plant placed close to the wall will need considerable watering until it has established roots that reach a reasonable distance away. It is often wiser to plant some little distance from the wall, say 40 cm (15 in) at least, and then to lead the top growth back, to allow it to climb.

WALL SHRUBS AND CLIMBERS

This is a short list of worthwhile kinds.

Actinidia kolomikta
Deciduous climber with foliage coloured green, white, cream and pink. Round white flowers appear in early summer. Suitable for sheltered wall or fence. Height 2–3.5 m (6–12 ft).

Camellia
Evergreens with good dark shiny foliage. There are hundreds of cultivars, bearing white, pink, or red flowers in late winter or spring. Plants enjoy an acid to neutral soil and in colder parts will like the more sheltered walls. Many will grow to about 3 m (10 ft) high.

Ceanothus
Evergreen and deciduous shrubs, which can be tailored to grow up a wall to almost any height or width. The mass of small dark leaves can be almost lost behind masses of blue flowers which appear for many weeks during summer. Of many kinds *C.* × 'Burkwoodii', *C.* 'Delight' and *C.* × 'Gloire de Versailles' are especially good.

Clematis
Deciduous climbers, ranging from popular species like the early small-flowered *C. montana*, to the large-flowered 'Jackmanii' and other hybrids that bloom from early summer into the late autumn. Flower colour range is from purple, blue, pink and red, through to white and yellow. Clematis can be grown up through other plants to give at least two seasons of colour and interest. Many are worth growing just for their foliage which, in the case of *C. tangutica*, can be almost fern-like. Flowers of this species are produced in succession from late summer until the frost, with buds like hanging lanterns, and four-petalled golden yellow flowers hanging like bells, followed by large silky seed heads. It will grow rapidly in any healthy soil.

Cotoneaster
The most popular species is the deciduous *C. horizontalis* with its herring-bone pattern of branches. It presses against the wall and often looks neat. Its rosy flowers of spring are followed by bright red berries in autumn but lasting well into winter. Others with later berries can be pruned to the wall. *C. lacteus* is one with lots of large durable berries.

Cytisus battandierii
From Morocco, this big-leaved broom with silky foliage and many large, tight bunches of yellow flowers is a quick-growing distinctive shrub that will grow well in the open but enjoys the support and shelter of a wall. The pineapple scent of the flowers, which appear in late spring and early summer, is always a surprise. Height of up to 4 m (15 ft).

Garrya elliptica
The rather dull, dark evergreen leaves build a rounded shape that is festooned through the autumn and winter months with very long, silvery grey-green catkins that make it a most decorative item at a difficult time in the garden. Height 3 m (10 ft) after 10 years.

Hedera (ivy)
The number of hardy evergreen ivies runs into hundreds. Brightly variegated ones are very decorative at all times, the small-leaved *H. helix* 'Goldheart' being very popular, but the large-leaved *H. canariensis* 'Variegata' and *H. colchica*

'Dentata Variegata' are perhaps even more opulent and impressive where space allows.

Jasminum nudiflorum (winter-flowering jasmine)

The winter jasmine, with its long dark green wands crowded with primrose yellow flowers in late autumn and winter, is something every garden would welcome. Its lax branches need to be supported and helped up the wall.

Lonicera (honeysuckle)

The climbing honeysuckles include the widely planted forms of the wild kind, the 'Early Dutch' and the later *L. periclymenum* 'Serotina' with purple-red and yellow flowers, but also the strong growing *L. americana* with flower bunches 30 cm (1 ft) across, and *L. japonica* 'Aureo-reticulata' with the rounded leaves netted with golden veining.

Pyracantha

Evergreen shrubs which can be grown in the open but are best tightly pruned against a wall where they can display their masses of berries for months in the autumn and winter. There are deep orange-red, tangerine-orange, and golden cultivars.

Roses

There are all sorts of climbing and rambling roses that can be grown on house walls. Once established they can form a framework for clambering clematis and other climbers.

Wisteria

Every cultivar is lovely but most take several years to get established and to bloom freely. There are some that bloom as very young specimens, *W. sinensis* 'Prematura' has the typical long grape-like bunches of purple-mauve flowers, and there is a white form, 'Prematura Alba'.

The twenty-first century is likely to see greater emphasis put on all things natural. The garden is the one place where an individual can help to create an atmosphere of natural tranquillity and beauty.

CHAPTER 3

WOODLAND, ONE-TREE WOODLANDS

Very few of us own stretches of woodland, but even a modest suburban garden can create the essential elements of this environment. Even a few square yards of a woodland atmosphere can add hugely to the interest and magic of the garden.

If nature was allowed its head, Britain would return to being a country almost wholly covered with trees. Many of our popular garden plants originally grew in woodland or in the flora-rich woodland edge. Our gardens often nearly reproduce the conditions of the woodland edge, with a scattering of trees, plenty of shrubs and, below, bulbs and other herbaceous plants. The amount of shade produced by trees will govern what grows below. Nothing grows under thick conifers, but below a wild ash or the golden *Robinia pseudoacacia* 'Frisia', where the shade is light and rain is not turned away, a rich mixture of plants will flourish. Birches allow light and rain but their extensive, shallow root system is so greedy and efficient that only a more limited association of plants will manage below.

The true woodland plant will probably favour a soil on the acid side of neutral. Leaves dropped by the trees rot and build up a humus-rich topsoil that will be on the acid side even where trees are growing on chalky alkaline soils. Many plants growing in woodland, or on their edges, are ones likely to want to get their growing done before the leaf canopy becomes too dense and shuts out rain and light. The wild daffodils, wood anemones and bluebells are obvious examples.

At its most restricted, our woodland garden will consist of a single tree with a supporting community of plants below. Aesthetically and atmospherically trees are important; we need something growing above our heads so that physically we enter an enveloping environment. In the suburban or smaller garden setting, the trees we use will be the smaller ones like cherry, apple, and thorn species. Of course, if you have the space to plant more than one tree, there is no doubt that three will more than treble the effect.

The choice of shrubs and climbing plants will depend on personal preferences. Some gardeners like to maximize drama with plenty of bright colourings; others will be happier with a more subdued picture and an effect not far removed from a corner of our natural countryside. How much we will want to continue manipulating the woodland scene once it is established will also depend on the garden owner. Some with a leaning towards conservation will allow wild plants – even an odd clump of nettles – for the benefit of butterfly and other insect life. However, even a clump of nettles requires management, as it is the young foliage that is attractive to most insects, and the time when some butterfly larvae need this can be later in the year than it naturally appears, so part of the clump will need cutting to produce fresh later young growth.

Within our patch of woodland can be created a complete ecosystem, with nesting and visiting birds, and even squirrels, foxes, hedgehogs and field mice. Bird and bat boxes may be installed along with suitable habitats arranged for other potential denizens.

DESIGN FACTORS

The planting of trees and shrubs has a major influence on the character of a garden. They may well be positioned to give the idea of a natural glade, but also serve to mask unsightly objects or vistas. They enhance the natural effect.

A balance of deciduous and evergreen species ensures that after leaf-fall the garden is not left looking like a bare stage. There are numerous cultivars of conifer that do not grow too large for the smaller garden; even the *Chamaecyparis lawsoniana* cultivars, which can eventually make very tall trees, are probably acceptable as they will take very many years to outgrow their site. Some, like the cultivar 'Lane', are a cheerful golden colour on the ends of their leaf fans and so have a brightening effect all year round.

Other evergreen trees play a slightly different role. The hardier eucalyptus species are interesting at all times. Hollies are slow-growing to start with, but once established can put on considerable growth each season. They are excellent hedge plants, can be grown as large screening trees, and females have the bonus of producing berries if there is a male specimen around to fertilize the flowers. Against a wall the evergreen *Magnolia grandiflora* is very impressive, with very large oval leaves that are highly lacquered and with their undersides coloured a rich brown. The large white flowers are an exciting bonus. *Arbutus unedo* (the strawberry tree) is found growing wild in south-west Ireland, and forms a cloud-shaped shrub that eventually may become a small tree. However, *A. menziesii* is more truly a tree. It has large oval, tough, dark leaves with very striking bright orange-red older branches and pyramids of flowers at the ends of its shoots. The colour is a creamy white and the shape the closed bell form of heathers.

Weeping willows are tempting but only where there is plenty of room. Other willows are more manageable. A popular kind is *Salix matsudana* 'Tortuosa' (the corkscrew willow), with every stem curling in many directions and contriving to make a silhouette that cuts a thousand jigsaw pieces out of the sky. It makes a graceful tree that can be cut back if it gets too large, but it needs siting with care as it has the annoying habit of dropping bits of dead twigs, and it takes a long time to disrobe at the end of the year.

Contrasting foliage creating a picture and covering the ground just as nature would dictate. Weeds are kept at bay with a layer of shredded bark. Hostas and a verbascum are in the foreground, ligularias and *Iris sibirica* in the middle ground with *Sambucus nigra* 'Aurea' (golden elder) and other shrubs to the rear.

CHOICE OF TREES

A garden of modest size is assumed; no huge trees are listed though some slow growers will eventually be tall.

Acer (maple)

Acers are deciduous and include huge trees such as the sycamores, which should be avoided. In contrast, many of the beautiful-leaved Japanese maples are very slow growing and will remain the size of shrubs for 10–15 years before slowly becoming small trees. They do best in well-drained soil that does not dry out. *A. palmatum* and *A. japonicum* prefer neutral or slightly acid soils. Other very attractive acers include:

A. davidii   This has interesting striped bark, grey on green. Five-pointed leaves turn bright golds, oranges and reds in autumn. Slow to 9 m (30 ft).

A. griseum   The paper-bark maple, so called for the showy way its rusty brown bark peels away to show orange-brown stems below. Typical maple leaves with pointing, deeply divided lobes turn bright colours before falling. Eventually 10 m (35 ft), but even small specimens are attractive.

A. japonicum   Of the many good cultivars, *A.j.* 'Aureum', with wide many-pointed fan-like leaves of bright yellow, is one of the most lovely. Slow to 6 m (20 ft).

A. palmatum   Japanese maple that makes a bush or small tree with five-pointed leaves. Some kinds, like the green 'Dissectum', or the crimson 'Dissectum Atropurpureum', have finely cut leaves almost like ferns. They spend most of their life as shrubs. Height up to 4.5 m (15 ft).

Arbutus (strawberry tree)

Dark-leaved evergreens making rounded cloud-shaped shrubs or small trees. *A. unedo* is the strawberry tree whose flower sprays in the autumn are rather like those of lily-of-the-valley. At the same time there are the round pimply orange-red 'strawberries' resulting from last year's flowers. 4.5–6 m (15–20 ft).

Betula (birch)

B. pendula is the silver birch of our countryside, which may or may not be pendulous. There are many named varieties. 'Laciniata' is a narrow tree with hanging twigs and leaves finely cut. 12 m (40 ft). 'Youngii' (Young's weeping birch) is the hunch-backed dwarf tree with branches falling straight down. 2.5 m.

B. utilis 'Jacquemontii' is a spectacular robust triangular tree with very vivid white bark on its trunk and stems. In winter particularly it looks as if it has been painted. 12 m (40 ft).

Chamaecyparis (formerly Cupressus)

C. lawsoniana (Lawson cypress) is basically a narrow conical tree that eventually can reach 30 m (100 ft), but many of the attractive forms are slow growing and will never reach these dizzy heights. 'Allumii' is often sold as a dwarf but slowly grows to 12 m (40 ft) making a wide deep blue-green column. 'Columnaris' is much narrower, taller, and blue-green. 'Ellwoodii' is a slow growing small cultivar making tight columns of blue-grey. 'Ellwood's Gold' is similar but with a golden cast as if caught by sunlight; eventually it makes a substantial tree, but takes a long time about it. 'Pembury Blue' is one of the best of the blue-green kinds. As a contrast 'Lane' is a bright gold, with darker green in the recesses of the fanned branches. It makes a good specimen tree.

Eucalyptus (gum tree)
Some of the 600 known kinds are hardier in Britain than previously thought. They are evergreen and may be purchased as young plants or easily raised from seed. Some species can grow from seed to 1.5 m (5 ft) in their first year. They grow on almost any soil with reasonable drainage.

E. gunnii This is the popular kind with very round young leaves closely clasped to the stem. It is much used by flower arrangers. Trees can be allowed to grow naturally quite high, when they will quickly assume their long pointed adult foliage, or they can be cut to the ground every two years or so in mid-spring and kept as a shrub – a fountain of silvery wands. It is sometimes too quick to make top growth so it is best to ensure a good root-run and hold on the earth, by cutting back your young specimen after one or two years' growth and allowing one or more trunks to grow.

E. nicholii is a delightful graceful tree with very narrow long leaves and somewhat pendant, very thin branches. Twigs are coloured red and the young foliage shades of orange.

E. niphophila (alpine snow gum) is extremely hardy with long pointed spear-shaped leaves hanging from slender branches. Trunks are silvered, the silver curling off older portions to reveal patterns of olive and buff. Height up to 6 m (20 ft).

Halesia (snowdrop tree)
H. carolina makes a pleasant tree, eventually after many years growing to 9 m (30 ft). It covers itself in late spring with many clusters of creamy white, hanging 'snowdrop' flowers. It does best on good sandy loam but will be almost as good on other soils.

Ilex (holly)
Whilst many hollies can eventually become tall trees, they are easily kept within bounds and are some of the best of all evergreens. Their polished richly coloured foliage always looks healthy and is especially welcome in winter. Particularly good are the better variegated kinds. 'Golden Queen' is broadly and brightly edged with creamy gold, 'Silver Queen' is equally good but with paler variegation. Height up to 5.5 m (18 ft).

Laburnum

With its long hanging tassels of bright golden pea flowers in late spring and early summer, all the laburnums are good value, but the most splendid is the hybrid *L. × watereri* 'Vossii' with very long, tapering bunches of flowers. Trees look mature at 5 m (15 ft) but can reach 6 m (20 ft) before looking ancient.

Magnolia

No magnolia is less than magnificent in bloom. Most popular in smaller gardens are the hybrids grouped under the name *M. × soulangeana*. These have the huge upright goblet flowers in various colours from pure white to very deep maroon. They begin to open before there is any hint of foliage but can last until the first leaves begin to unfurl. Part of their popularity is due to the fact that even small specimens will carry a good quota of flowers. 'Lennei' is rosy purple outside but white inside. 'Rustica Rubra' is a rich pinky purple. 'Alba Superba' and 'Lennei Alba' are both very impressive and almost pure white. Height 3–4.5 m (10–15 ft).

Malus (crab apple)

The apple species can make most spectacular trees, often living to a good long age without becoming too large. Some have deep purple leaves as well as a mass of pinky red flowers and dark maroon crab apples. 'Aldenhamensis' is one of these, growing only to about 4.5 m (15 ft). 'Eleyi' grows a little taller and produces masses of tiny, long-stemmed, dark apples.

M. floribunda is a most lovely flowering species, green leaved, in spring producing a cloud of blossom made up of rich carmine buds and open white flowers. It is difficult to see how it could fit another flower into the mass. It has small red fruit. Trees grow in a circumspect manner up to 9 m (30 ft). In autumn and through much of the winter the hybrid 'Golden Hornet' is festooned with shining golden crab apples.

Prunus (cherry)

Most of the *Prunus* genus are highly decorative deciduous trees of modest height, but there are evergreens such as the hedging plants *P. laurocerasus* (common laurel) and *P. lusitanicus* (Portugal laurel). The genus includes almonds as well as all the flowering and fruiting cherries.

P. subhirtella 'Autumnalis' (winter-flowering cherry) is well worth a place as it makes a pleasing, spreading, somewhat pendulous tree with medium-sized foliage that turns orange shades in the autumn, when it starts blooming. Showers of small pale pink or white blossom are carried through the milder weather of winter until spring. It will allow plenty of undergrowth of other plants and makes an ideal tree for natural gardening. It also blends more effectively than some of the blatant Japanese flowering cherries.

P. 'Kanzan' is the ubiquitous double pink kind with rather upright branching habit. Quite different is 'Mount Fuji' (Shirotae) with wide spreading, almost

A happy association of the white-stemmed *Eucalyptus niphophila* with the butterfly's favourite, *Sedum spectabile*, and a fern, *Dryopteris filix-mas* 'Mapplebeck'.

horizontal branches and large white hanging flowers. 'Spire' and 'Amanogawa' are small trees of tight, upright, fastigiate stance; the branches hug each other and in spring are decorated with pink blossom.

Pyrus (pear)

Many of the deciduous pears make wonderful specimen trees, the hybrids grown for their fruit as well as the wild species. In much demand now is the willow-leaved pear, *P. salicifolia*, with its narrow silvery leaves and white flowers. It will take a long time to outgrow its usual 3.5–4.5 m (12–15 ft) to reach a possible ultimate height of 7.5 m (25 ft). It makes a mass of growth so that the head is a tangle of branches, many hanging down to give a pendulous effect.

Rhus (sumach)

These shrubs that grow into small trees make wide-angled thick-stemmed deciduous frameworks for leaves, pinnate like those of the ash tree. *R. typhina* 'Laciniata' is made more attractive by each leaflet being deeply cut. Quite early in the autumn the leaves turn brilliant shades of orange and red. It allows plenty of plant growth below.

Sorbus (whitebeam and mountain ash)

S. aria is the common whitebeam, a very neat deciduous tree that looks especially fine in the spring when its wide leaves emerge from silky white buds. It can keep this silken appearance for a long time before wearing down to a rich dark green, though often still furry white below. The spring bunches of white flowers, rather like late spring snowfall, can be followed in autumn by red and brown fruits that the birds usually pick off. Height 4.5–6 m (15–20 ft).

S. aucuparia is the wild rowan or mountain ash. It can be rather slow to grow but once established there are few small trees more decorative, with their huge bunches of orange-red fruits from late summer till the winter. There are yellow-fruited forms such as 'Fructo Luteo'. Height 4.5–7.5 m (15–25 ft).

S. hupehensis is a delightful little tree with ferny foliage, each leaf being made up of many small leaflets. Berries are white, turning to mauvey pink with age. This is one of the best trees for the very small garden, as it hardly ever gets much beyond 4.5 m (15 ft).

PLANTING

Suggestions follow for group plantings based on a single main tree. You can follow one plan or try amalgamating a few ideas.

ONE-TREE WOODLAND 1 (Fig. 4)

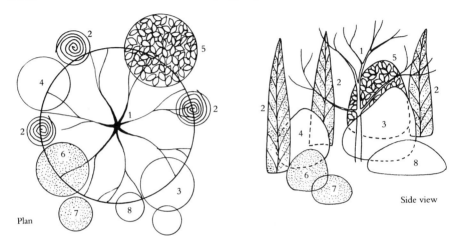

Fig. 4 One-tree Woodland 1: 1. *Prunus.* 2. *Juniperus* 'Skyrocket'. 3. *Cotinus coggygria.* 4. *Ribes sanguineum.* 5. *Viburnum tinus.* 6. *Mahonia.* 7. *Santolina.* 8. *Genista.*

Soil: ordinary, perhaps poor.

Lead tree: *Prunus subhirtella* 'Autumnalis' or other prunus.

Supporting cast:
Juniperus 'Skyrocket'.
Cotinus coggygria, purple-leaved form, e.g. 'Royal Purple'.
Ribes sanguineum 'Brocklebankii'.
Viburnum tinus 'Eve Price'.
Mahonia aquifolium (Oregon grape), *M. japonica,* or *M. × media* 'Charity'.
Santolina chamaecyparissus (lavender cotton)
Genista hispanica, or double gorse or brooms.

Character of planting There is a contrast between the widespread deciduous form of the prunus and the upright columns of fastigiate junipers. Yews or other conifers could play the upright role. *Ribes sanguineum* 'Brocklebankii' has golden foliage shown up by the evergreen *Viburnum tinus,* junipers and mahonias.

Further contrast is offered by the reddish purple *Cotinus*, but this could be done by the smaller *Berberis thunbergii* 'Atropurpurea'. Supplementary plantings of brooms will give quick spring and summer colour. It is sometimes possible to lead climbers like honeysuckle into the cherry.

Underplanting A wide range of bulbs can be planted for early spring effect. *Cyclamen hederifolium* in good numbers will give autumn colour, followed by attractive winter and spring foliage. Epimediums and tiarellas can be added for foliage groundcover. Heathers would also look well.

ONE-TREE WOODLAND 2 (Fig. 5)

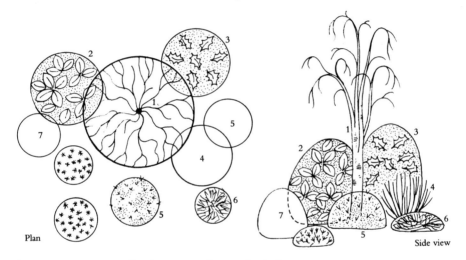

Fig. 5 One-tree Woodland 2: 1. *Betula*. 2. Rhododendron. 3. *Ilex*. 4. *Viburnum bodnantense*. 5. *Genista/ Ulex*. 6. *Juniperus*. 7. *Weigela*.

Soil: Acid, possibly dryish.

Lead tree: *Betula pendula* (native silver birch) or any other species.

Supporting cast:
Rhododendron, large-flowered hybrid such as 'Britannia' (red) or 'Pink Pearl'.
Ilex (holly), green or variegated cultivar according to taste.
Viburnum bodnantense 'Dawn' or *V. farrerii*.
Genista (broom) or *Ulex* (gorse).
Juniperus, prostrate forms such as *J. × media* 'Pfitzeriana Aurea'.
Weigela florida 'Aureovariegata' or *Deutzia* such as 'Mont Rose' or *D. scabra* 'Flore Pleno'.

Character of planting Dominated by one, or a group of three birches. A moorland flavour suggested by gorse and heathers. Rhododendrons and hollies add gravitas, with their heavy evergreen colour contrasting with the light, graceful feel of the silvery-barked birches. Conifers could be included. Lower plants such as andomedas, gaultherias, sarcococcas, and other heather relatives could be added to emphasize the heathland atmosphere.

Underplanting Lily-of-the-valley and small bulbs add to the interest. Clumps of reeds or grasses such as *Luzula sylvatica* 'Marginata' and 'Bowles Golden Sedge' could also be added, as well as smaller flowers such as the various violets, woodruff, and geranium species. One or two of the stronger ferns would help provide variety.

ONE-TREE WOODLAND 3 (Fig. 6)

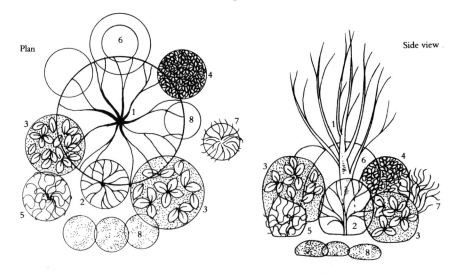

Fig. 6 One-tree Woodland 3: 1. *Carpinus*. 2. *Hamamelis*. 3. Rhododendrons. 4. Camellia. 5. *Corylus*. 6. *Philadelphus*. 7. *Rosa*. 8. Heathers.

Soil: Somewhat acid.

Lead tree: *Carpinus betulus* 'Fastigiata' (fastigiate hornbeam).

Supporting cast:
Hamamelis mollis (witch hazel) or hybrids.
Rhododendron, large-flowered hybrids.

Camellia japonica or *C. reticulata* hybrid.
Corylus avellana 'Contorta' (corkscrew hazel).
Philadelphus (mock orange) 'Virginal' or other hybrid.
Rosa, rambling hybrid or species, or shrub rose like 'Canary Bird'.
Heathers.

Character of planting Upright lines of fastigiate deciduous tree contrast with dark evergreen of rhododendrons and camellias. Witch hazel's winter bloom shows up against dark rhododendrons. Twisted stems of corkscrew hazel emphasize the straight line of hornbeam and respectably clothed rhododendrons. One or more rambling roses may be led into branches of hornbeam.

Underplanting It could be possible to get the creeping dogwood, *Cornus canadensis*, going through leafy soil. Heathers and other ericaceous plants may be added. In addition to plenty of spring bulbs, try to find a place for bold clumps of *Lilium pyrenaicum* and later *L. pardalinum giganteum* (leopard lily). Hostas and ferns could feature extensively at ground level.

Heathers, gorses, philadelphus and such shrubs will carry the burden of interest through earlier years until the rhododendrons and camellias get to a reasonable size.

ONE-TREE WOODLAND 4 (Fig. 7)

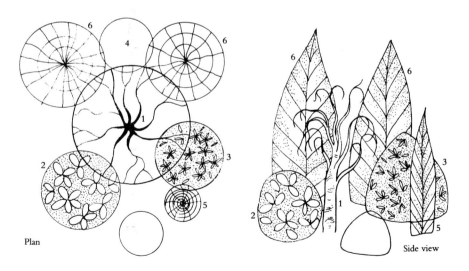

Fig. 7 One-tree Woodland 4: 1. *Laburnum*. 2. *Aucuba*. 3. *Arbutus*. 4. *Cornus*. 5. *Juniperus*. 6. *Cupressocyparis*.

Soil: Definitely limy. Drainage adequate.

Lead tree: *Laburnum × watereri* 'Vossii'.

Supporting cast:
Aucuba japonica 'Variegata' (spotted laurel).
Arbutus unedo (strawberry tree) or *A. × andrachnoides.*
Cornus mas (cornelian cherry), winter-flowering dogwood.
Juniperus 'Skyrocket'.
Cupressocyparis 'Castlewellan Gold' (golden leylandii).

Character of planting The lead tree grows quickly, as will the conifers. *Arbutus* and *Cornus* will be slow. A certain amount of filling in will have to be undertaken with quick-maturing shrubs such as tree lupins, brooms, philadelphus species and hybrids, weigelas or deutzias. A variety of hardy hebes will contribute foliage round the year.

Underplanting Bold foliage effect can be achieved by using acanthus; slightly lighter will be aconitums (monkshood). Thalictrums can rival some ferns in foliar effect. Hellebores can give foliage and flower particularly in winter and early spring months. *Symphytum grandiflorum* (little comfrey) and *Lamium maculatum* (variegated dead nettle) can act as ground cover. Cyclamens will be at home on lime and so will all the real geraniums.

ONE-TREE WOODLAND 5 (Fig. 8)

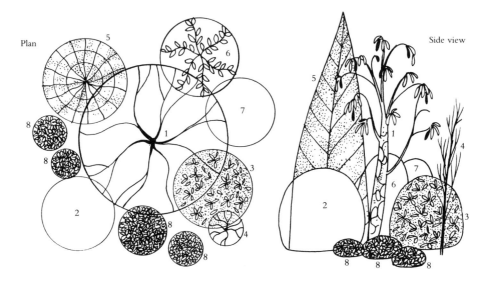

Soil: Reasonably drained.

Lead tree: *Eucalyptus gunnii* or *E. niphophila.*

Supporting cast:
Cotinus coggygria 'Royal Purple'.
Olearia × haastii (daisy bush).
Prunus 'Spire' or 'Amanogawa'.
Cupressocyparis 'Castlewellan Gold'.
Cotoneaster × watereri 'Cornubia'.
Forsythia 'Lynwood'.
Hebe, various hardy kinds such as *H. pinguifolia* 'Pagei'.

Character of planting The lead tree gives us the clue. Here we are aiming at something a little different. Either a single eucalyptus, or a closely planted group of three, will grow fast and soon make a significant impact. *Olearia × haastii* from New Zealand will give a crop of white summer blossom and twelve months' worth of rich green to add to the eucalypt's silver-grey. Purple-red from the deciduous *Cotinus* adds drama. Conifer 'Castlewellan Gold' provides contrasting colour. A selection of small and large hebes will take the place normally filled by heathers. Good winter berries will be the tall-reaching cotoneaster's gift. Forsythias, deutzias, *Senecio* 'Sunshine', and philadelphus can be added for more immediate effect.

Underplanting Creeping acaenas from New Zealand can form part of the groundcover. Other low plants like pachysandras and epimediums can also play a part. Ferns can be added to accentuate the unusual atmosphere. Bulbs of all hardy sorts can be popped in for spring, summer and autumn colour.

Opposite:
Fig. 8 One-tree Woodland 5: 1. *Eucalyptus*. 2. *Cotinus*. 3. *Olearia*. 4. *Prunus*. 5. *Cupressocyparis*. 6. *Cotoneaster*. 7. *Forsythia*. 8. *Hebe*.

ONE-TREE WOODLAND 6 (Fig. 9)

Fig. 9 One-tree Woodland 6: 1. *Catalpa*. 2. *Viburnum* 'Eve Price.' 3. *Viburnum* 'Dawn'. 4. *Cornus alba*. 5. *Cornus stolonifera*. 6. *Juniperus* 7. Evergreen (hollies, conifers).

Soil: Wide area needed.

Lead tree: *Catalpa bignonioides* 'Aurea' (golden Indian bean tree).

Supporting cast:
Viburnum tinus 'Eve Price'.
V. farrerii or *V. bodnantense* 'Dawn'.
Cornus alba 'Elegantissima' and/or *C.a.* 'Westonbirt' (dogwood).
C. stolonifera 'Flaviramea' (dogwood).
Juniperus, prostrate forms, such as *J. horizontalis* cultivars.
Evergreens, yews, hollies, or quick-growing conifers such as some of the *Chamaecyparis lawsoniana* series, or *Cupressocyparis leylandii*.

Character of planting Major summertime effect from large pale golden leaves of widespread spare-branched Indian bean tree. This will eventually make a large broad shape. It looks best seen against a dark background and with shelter offered by substantial evergreens. Virburnums, together with dogwoods, provide winter colour. Forsythias, lavenders, philadelphus hybrids, *Senecio* 'Sunshine', and *Potentilla fruticosa* forms can all help with early colour and form whilst the major actors are growing into their roles.

Underplanting Contrasting foliage plants such as hostas and ferns can be given extra colour and form with acanthus, aconitums, foxgloves and bergenias. Spring and autumn can be made special festivals with lots of small daffodils and autumn-blooming crocuses, cyclamens and colchicums.

ONE-TREE WOODLAND 7 (Fig. 10)

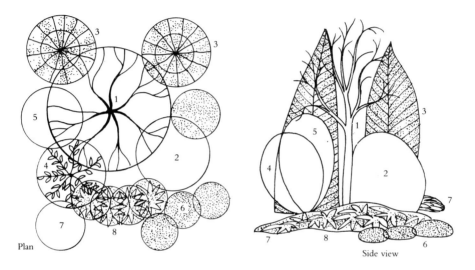

Fig. 10 One-tree Woodland 7: 1. *Robinia*. 2. *Cotinus*. 3. Evergreens (hollies, yews etc.) 4. *Cotoneaster*. 5. *Cytisus*. 6. Heathers. 7. *Cotoneaster dammerii*. 8. *Juniperus*.

Soil: Reasonable drainage, unexciting soil.

Lead tree: *Robinia pseudoacacia* 'Frisia'.

Supporting cast:
Cotinus coggygria 'Royal Purple' or *Berberis thunbergii* 'Atropurpurea'.
Evergreens such as *Chamaecyparis* species, hollies or yews.
Cotoneaster frigida, or similar larger species.
Cytisus battandierii.
Heathers.
Cotoneaster dammerii 'Gnome' or similar ground-hugging dwarf.
Juniperus sabina 'Tamariscifolia' or similar prostrate blue-grey.
Euphorbias (spurges), hostas, bulbs.

ONE-TREE WOODLAND 8 (Fig. 11)

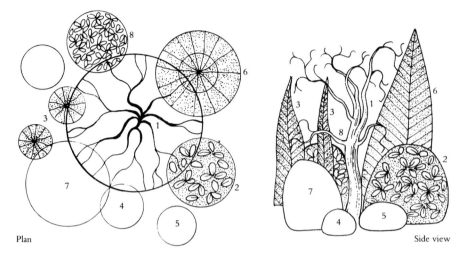

Plan   Side view

Fig 11 One–tree Woodland 8: 1. *Salix*. 2. *Aucuba*. 3. *Juniperus*. 4. *Potentilla*.
5. *Hypericum*. 6. *Chamaecyparis*. 7. *Corylus*. 8. *Rhododendron*.

Soil: Possibly moist, but away from house as falling leaves of willow can be annoying.

Lead tree: *Salix matsudana* 'Tortuosa' (corkscrew willow).

Supporting cast:
Aucuba japonica 'Variegata' (spotted laurel)
Juniperus 'Skyrocket' or *J. hibernica*.
Potentilla fruticosa forms.
Hypericum 'Hidcote'.
Chamaecyparis lawsoniana 'Pembury Blue', 'Lane' or similar.
Corylus maxima 'Purpurea' (purple hazel).
Rhododendron, large–flowered hybrids.

ONE-TREE WOODLAND 9 (Fig. 12)

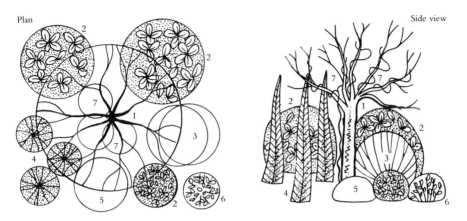

Fig. 12 One-tree Woodland 9: 1. Apple, Pear or Cherry. 2. Rhododendrons. 3. *Cornus*. 4. *Juniperus*. 5. *Daphne*. 6. *Ruscus*. 7. Climber.

Soil: Acid, reasonably drained.

Lead tree: *Malus*, *Pyrus*, or *Prunus* (apple, pear, or cherry).

Supporting cast:
Rhododendron, large and small types.
Cornus 'Westonbirt' (red dogwood).
Juniperus hibernica or similar columnar form.
Daphne mezereum and *D. laureola* (spurge laurel).
Ruscus aculeatus (butcher's broom).
Climbers, various: clematis, honeysuckles, vines etc.

ONE-TREE WOODLAND 10 (Fig. 13)

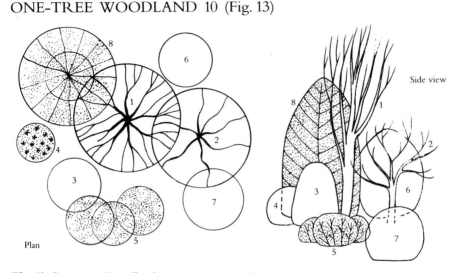

Fig 13 One-tree Woodland 10: 1. *Fagus*. 2. *Rhus*. 3. *Cytisus*. 4. *Rosmarinus*. 5. *Genista*. 6. *Caragana*. 7. *Atriplex*. 8. *Taxus*.

Soil: Rather dry.

Lead tree: *Fagus sylvatica* 'Dawyck' (fastigiate beech).

Supporting cast:
Rhus typhina (stag's horn sumach).
Cytisus battandieri (Moroccan pineapple broom).
Rosmarinus officinalis (rosemary).
Genista hispanica (Spanish gorse).
Caragana arborescens (pea tree).
Atriplex halimus (tree purslane).
Taxus baccata (yew).
Spring bulbs, plus *Gladiolus byzantinus*, *Nerine bowdenii*, *Colchicum* species and hybrids, hardy *Cyclamen* species.
Euphorbia, *Brunnera*, *Pulmonaria*, *Alchemilla*, *Geum*.

In semi-woodland conditions there are a number of attractive plants that will naturalize themselves by seed and look well with no effort from the gardener. The biennial honesty can make wide drifts in very dry soils where very little else grows. The masses of purple-mauve flowers in early summer are followed by the flat seed head that glistens through autumn and winter. Foxgloves, in all shades from the usual pink mauve to darker maroons and to whites, creams, and yellows, will look distinctive through the summer. It produces millions of fertile seeds so that reproduction is no problem. The same can be said of the aquilegias, either long- or short-spurred, coming in all sorts of colours – whites, blues, pinks, reds and golds, and some attractively bi-coloured ones. The steel grey foliage, rather like magnified maidenhair fern, looks well throughout the growing period. To begin the naturalizing process, seeds can either be broadcast where they are to colonize, or plants can be raised under glass, potted off and planted out when established so that they have a head start.

CHAPTER 4

THE ROLE OF SHRUBS

Shrubs usually form the backbone of the natural garden. They give it permanent shape and are on duty twelve months of the year. Most can be left to get on with their own devices, without much overseeing from the gardener beyond dealing with any invasive weeds. Occasionally branches may have to be pruned – those that have died, or are obviously misplaced and perhaps spoiling the shape of the whole. But shrubs believe in self-help; they will often smother weeds and will help to retain a reasonable soil structure.

ACID SOILS

Choice of shrubs will depend on what the gardener wishes to achieve, as well as the type of soil in the garden. On decidedly acid soils it would be perverse not to make use of some of the many rhododendrons that will flourish. Of course the choice amongst these is almost bewildering, ranging from tiny hummocks of small leaves, which belong to the mountain-top species that delight the alpine enthusiast, to other kinds that grow into substantial trees. Between these there are the majority of species and hybrids, some with huge trusses of flowers and others covering themselves with lots of smaller blooms.

There are many natural companion shrubs for rhododendrons, including other members of the very large ericaceous family. Heathers are excellent for a heathland atmosphere and if you plant a collection there can be colour all round the year. Young plants will soon be paying their rent and willingly bear the brunt of the show whilst the larger plants are growing. *Erica carnea* is unusual in being lime tolerant and in its many cultivars can be in bloom from early autumn till mid-spring. *Calluna vulgaris* has produced a very long line of distinct plants, many of which are not only gorgeous in bloom for many summer weeks but have attractively coloured foliage. They are excellent plants for the natural garden, look an integral part of the scene if planted with a little imagination, and once growing well will do their utmost to keep themselves weed free.

There are other heather relatives that scarcely look like heathers, being larger and handsomely leaved. Amongst these the *Pieris* forms are excellent value plants. These have lots of creamy white sprays of flowers, like transplanted lily-of-the-valley blossom, but they also have evergreen, polished, clean-looking rich green leaves that start life as young unfurling shoots in lovely orange, red, pink and tan shades. The colour of the young foliage lasts for several weeks and in some cultivars is more brilliant than many vaunted flower displays. *Pieris* 'Forest Flame' is the most widely available of many very fine kinds. Its young foliage certainly sets light to the bush, with deep carmine pinks and reds jockeying with other shades for prominence. Eventually the leaves mature to green but this takes a long time.

Forms of *Cytisus* and *Genista* (broom) and *Ulex* (gorse) are very quick growing and spectacular in bloom. They have typical pea flowers and will cover themselves with blossom. From a large number, the early *Cytisus praecox* makes a more or less upright rounded bush of bright green, turning to a foaming mass of cream in spring. 'Allgold' is dwarfer and a rich golden yellow. *C. purpureus* is different, with lilac-purple flowers smothering low-spreading bushes. The native *C. scoparius* has many named cultivars, including many rich reds or bi-colours of cream or yellow and red.

Genista hispanica (Spanish broom) is a very worthwhile plant that makes dense, rounded, low sculptures of green, spread over with a golden cloth of bloom in the spring. *G. lydia* opens a little later and makes a looser but neat bright green bush of many slender growths that carry innumerable small pea flowers in brightest gold, so crowded as to make a complete cover.

Ulex europeus is our familiar well-armed gorse. *U.e.* 'Plenus' is a double-flowered form and makes a very fine garden shrub. It is particularly useful on very poor soil, and indeed it is a mistake to grow it too lushly as bits may die back. Grown on hard rations, it makes a very compact hedgehog shrub that looks distinct out of flower, and in bloom produces a mass of long lasting golden blossom.

LIMY SOILS

Whilst all the *Erica carnea* heathers flourish on neutral or limy soils, the *Cytisus* species generally do not like a lot of lime, although the hybrids seem more tolerant. *Genista hispanica* grows well on lime. Other shrubs, like viburnum, relish lime and are best in these types of soil. Of the many shrubs that are completely indifferent to the presence of lime, useful ones include the popular spring forsythia with its cloud of yellow blossom, the variously coloured chaenomeles, berberis, deutzia, philadelphus, buddleja, hydrangea, hebe, potentilla and cotoneaster.

Many shrubs, whilst ideally grown in soil slightly on the acid side, will manage with some lime without showing any distress. Most roses, for example, like soil just on the acid side of neutral but millions are grown happily in limy soils. In our shortlist of shrubs that do well in a natural garden setting, notes are made of soil preferences.

Winter-flowering heathers, colourful from autumn until well into spring, planted here where they will make the most impact in the dullest days. *Erica carnea* cultivars.

SHORTLIST OF SHRUBS

All of these make a significant contribution either in bloom, in their year-round character, or in some special way such as the witch hazels with their brilliant winter blossom.

Berberis Lime tolerant. Evergreen and deciduous spp. Sun/partial shade. Of many good species and hybrids, *B.* × *stenophylla* is outstanding in all its forms. It forms a thick evergreen bush of armed small leaves, which in spring are covered with masses of small orange–gold flowers.

Buddleja Enjoys lime. Deciduous. Sun.
B. davidii (butterfly bush) is the popular kind with long spikes of flowers in summer and autumn to attract the butterflies. There are dark purples, crimson purples and whites, as well as the familiar mauves. Slightly less tall and with rather smaller leaves is *B.d. nanhoensis* 'Nanho Blue', but do not be deceived by garden

centre labels suggesting that this only grows to about 1–1.2 m (3–4 ft), as it can double this easily.

Calluna Acid lover. Evergreen. Sun.
The wild heather or ling of Britain's countryside has produced many forms, and well over 200 are offered for sale.

Camellia Acid lover. Evergreen. Open/partial shade.
With highly polished, rich green oval leaves and round, very formal flowers, these are decidedly stylish plants, but acceptable in the natural garden and invaluable in acid soils. The early flowers are susceptible to early-morning frosts. Plant in warm sheltered areas.

Ceanothus Lime tolerant. Evergreen. Sun/partial shade.
Often grown as wall shrubs, either closely clipped or allowed to grow more informally, they enjoy the support of the wall and its warmth. This is one of the few genera rich in blue blossom. Small shiny leaves make a dark backcloth for innumerable tightly rounded heads of bright blue tiny flowers. There are many good species and hybrids. *C. impressus* and *C. dentatus* are popular. *C. repens* is a low-growing kind. 'A. T. Johnson', 'Autumnal Blue' and 'Cascade' are very free-flowering strong hybrids.

Chaenomeles Lime tolerant. Deciduous. Sun.
Still often known as 'cydonia' or simply 'japonica' these quinces are gloriously colourful in early months. They are particularly good against a wall, which by its warmth helps the wood to ripen thoroughly and to produce plenty of flowering buds. The red and orange blossom can start opening from mid-winter onwards. There are very attractive white and pink forms too. Early bees and insects make use of their pollen for food.

Colutea arborescens Lime tolerant. Dedicuous. Sun.
The common bladder senna is a strong deciduous shrub belonging to the pea family, as can be seen by its leaves of nine to thirteen leaflets and the golden yellow pea flowers. It grows quickly to perhaps 3–3.5 m (10–12 ft) and can seed itself from the pea seeds inside the inflated papery pods that are a feature of the tree/shrub.

Corylus Lime tolerant. Deciduous. Sun/partial shade.
One or two hazel cultivars are worth planting for their foliage. There is a bright form, *C. avellana* 'Aurea', with yellowy leaves that are brighter in spring and in full sun. The most spectacular of the purple-leaved varieties is *C. maxima* 'Purpurea', which has large, very dark maroon-purple leaves, made even larger if the shrub is cut back every two or three years.

Cotoneaster Lime tolerant. Evergreen and deciduous. Sun/partial shade.

These range from ground-hugging species like *C. dammeri*, through reaching types like the well-known *C. horizontalis* and *C. franchetii*, to kinds that can grow into small trees, such as the evergreen *C. × watereri* series that can look magnificent for months through the winter with huge crops of bunched red berries. All cotoneasters are easy plants that look after themselves. They are crowded with bees and other busy insects at flowering time, and when berried form a reserve food supply for many birds.

Deutzia Lime tolerant. Deciduous. Sun.

These are very easy quick-growing shrubs with trumpet-shaped flowers in a variety of colours from white to deep red.

Erica Lime tolerant/acid lovers. Evergreen. Sun.

E. carnea There are few more useful lime-tolerant species of heather than this. There is a range of cultivars, some which are rather lower growing such as 'Vivellii', with foliage almost black and dark red flowers, and others several times as high at 20–25 cm (8–10 in) such as pink-flowered 'King George'. There are also yellow-foliaged kinds, pink-flowered 'Foxhollow' being one of the best and most richly coloured in winter. Planted in as bold sweeps as possible, these heathers provide carpets of living colour from autumn till well into spring. They look natural, associate well with conifers, brooms, birches, gorses and other shrubs and bulbs, and by their thick growth suppress weed.

E. vagans, Cornish heath, will stand a little lime but is best in acid conditions. Cultivars bloom through late summer into the middle of autumn and, even when the flowers fade, the rusty dead heads still look attractive through the winter. 'Lyonesse' has white spikes contrasting with dark glossy foliage. 'Mrs Maxwell' is a rich rosy cultivar of tight growth.

E. cinerea is the Scotch bell heather which certainly hates lime. They have a long flowering season, many starting in mid-summer and still going strong well into autumn, to the time of the frosts. Purple-red flowers of 'Golden Hue' are secondary to the golden leaves that turn glowing orange-red in winter.

Forsythia Lime tolerant. Dedicuous. Sun/partial shade.

The masses of golden blossom that bedeck these shrubs before the leaves arrive are very dramatic. To get the very best results prune out the weaker wood and much of the old flowering wood immediately after flowering to encourage plenty of fresh growth for next season's bloom.

Garrya elliptica Lime tolerant. Evergreen. Sun/shade.

A dark rather dull green evergreen, festooned with fascinating silvery catkins through the winter.

Hebe Lime tolerant. Evergreen. Sun.

These are very variable and some of the more spectacularly flowered kinds with long bottle-brush spikes of flowers in purples, violets, pinks, blues may be cut back or even killed by a very severe winter. Others, such as the low-growing, spreading *H. pinguifolia* 'Pagei' makes a compact silvery mass of neatly arranged oval leaves impervious to the winter weather.

Hydrangea Lime tolerant. Deciduous. Sun/partial shade.

The large mop-headed hydrangea can look very impressive for months, but may seem a little artificial. Perhaps more natural and graceful are the 'lace-caps' such as 'Blue Wave', with each flower head having tiny inner flowers of purplish blue and an outer ring of large blooms that range from pink to blue, depending on the acidity of the soil.

Hypericum Lime tolerant. Deciduous. Sun.

Of the many kinds, *H.* 'Hidcote' is one of the showiest, with rounded bushes up to 1.2 m (4 ft) high and through, covered for the whole summer with saucer-shaped flowers in brilliant gold. It will do well even on very poor thin soils.

Jasminum Lime tolerant. Evergreen effect. Sun/partial shade.

The most important is *J. nudiflorum* (winter jasmine) with its dark green stems studded with lemon yellow flowers from late autumn till late winter. It can be grown sprawling over the ground, falling down a bank, or, as most often seen, encouraged to climb up a wall. It blooms more freely if given a trim after flowering so that a lot of new growth is made.

Juniperus Lime tolerant. Evergreen. Sun/partial shade.

There are many forms of these conifers. *J. chinensis* 'Pyramidalis' is an upright, soldierly, steel blue column up to 1.8 m (6 ft) high after 10 years, *J.* 'Gold Cone' is a narrow, bright yellow pillar only half as high in the same period. Of the spreading types, *J.* 'Pfitzeriana Aurea' is the popular and vigorous golden green kind, and *J. horizontalis* 'Blue Chip' is one of the best of the silvery blue cultivars, feathery in growth and making very low ground cover.

Ligustrum Lime tolerant. Evergreen/deciduous. Sun/shade.

L. ovalifolium 'Aureum' is the popular golden privet which is well worth growing as a specimen shrub for its year-round bright colour and to use for augmenting indoor arrangements.

Mahonia Lime tolerant. Evergreen. Sun/partial shade.

Whilst it is difficult to find a poor mahonia, some of the hybrids are outstanding for their distinguished-looking toothed, tough green leaves arranged in pinnate fashion like ash leaves, and also for the winter flowers atop each stem – bunches of spreading sprays of lemon-gold, scented blossoms from late autumn through the winter.

Philadelphus Lime tolerant. Deciduous. Sun/light shade.

The mock oranges are easy and very free-flowering bushes, which are good on even poor soils. 'Beauclerk' crowds bending branches with wide white flowers slightly flushed pink. 'Belle Etoile' has large single blooms of white but centred with a maroon blotch. 'Virginal', which can grow easily to 2.5 m (8 ft) high by 1.8 m (6 ft) wide, is a rather larger shrub and has heavily scented white double flowers.

Pieris Acid lover. Evergreen. Sun/partial shade.

Evergreens with sprays of white lily-of-the-valley flowers, but noted for the brilliant orange-red young foliage, as in 'Forest Flame'. There is also the bonus of the flower's fragrance.

Potentilla Lime tolerant. Deciduous. Sun.

The shrubby potentillas are very easy plants in an open situation with reasonable drainage. There are now many varieties, usually making rounded bushes soon reaching 75 cm (30 in) high and rather wider. They will continue in bloom from early summer till the frosts. 'Princess' is pink, 'Red Ace' a rich orange, 'Daydawn' a pinky yellow, 'Gold Drop' a rich yellow, and 'Tilford Cream' a white.

Rhododendron Acid lover. Evergreen. Partial shade/sun.

There are thousands of rhododendrons. Becoming more popular every year are the *R. yakushimanum* hybrids, commonly referred to as 'Yaks'. These are a fine series of compact low-growing plants with good healthy foliage that is virtually covered with large trusses of flowers. They are ideal for the smaller garden and for growing in containers. 'Percy Wiseman' is one of the leaders, with rich pink buds opening pink and cream and fading to pale cream. 'Grumpy' opens primrose and fades close to white. 'Sparkler' has bright crimson flowers and is particularly compact in growth.

Rhus Lime tolerant. Deciduous. Sun/partial shade.

R. typhina is the stag's horn sumach, a wide angled large shrub with its furry stems holding large pinnate leaves of many leaflets that turn brilliant orange and red in autumn. The tight-fisted crimson red flower spikes last well into the winter months.

Senecio Lime tolerant. Evergreen. Sun.

S. 'Sunshine' is a very useful spreading shrub with silvery oval leaves that look well at all times. It can almost smother itself with sprays of golden daisy flowers in mid-summer. This is a hardy shrub, able to grow well even in very poor and dry soils.

Opposite:
Hamamelis mollis, the witch hazel, in full bloom in the middle of the winter.

Viburnum Lime tolerant. Evergreen and deciduous. Sun/partial shade. These shrubs are some of the most useful of all, and if 'useful' seems a low-power adjective in the 'damning with faint praise' mould, such a slight is not intended. There are a few ordinary ones, but most can contribute handsomely to the garden scene whilst being very undemanding in culture. Many will grow well in poor sites and in this lies some of their usefulness. They are a hardy lot, with some exceptionally welcome for their durable winter blossom and most backing attractive floral displays with pleasing perfumes. Others are amongst the most spectacular of berrying shrubs.

Wild through Britain, Europe and North Africa the guelder rose, *V. opulus*, can be magnificent in autumn, with drooping wide bunches of oval 7 mm (⅓ in) fruits highly polished in a semi-translucent manner and of a vivid scarlet. They will hang after the red and orange display of autumn foliage has fallen. There is a brilliant golden form, *V.o. xanthocarpum*. Flowers are tiny white ones yellowed with anthers and in 7–8 cm (3 in) flat bunches, ringed with the larger milk-white infertile flowers in the manner of lace-cap hydrangeas. They make vigorous, rather leafy deciduous bushes up to 3–3.5 m (10–12 ft) high with lobed leaves looking like rather coarse-grained maples. Whilst they might be introduced into wilder areas of the garden and where collections of native plants are gathered, their place in smaller gardens may be taken by rather less extrovert types. The most planted of *V. opulus* forms is the snowball tree, *V.o.* 'Sterile', with flowering heads forced into large round balls by all the individual flowers being large infertile ones. They are creamy white when fresh, pleasantly limy green in youth, and fawn in old age.

Of the berrying kinds the deciduous *V. dilatum* is modestly attractive in June bloom, with white clusters 7–10 cm (3–4 in) across and not unpleasing with bright green foliage. But it is in autumn that it looks its best with rich foliage colours and many large clusters of rounded red fruits, or rich golden ones in the fine form *V.d. xanthocarpum*.

Amongst the deciduous viburnums it is *V. farreri* (*V. fragrans*) and its hybrids, with the more opulent but slightly tender *V. grandiflorum*, that are deservedly most popular. The hybrids, led by 'Dawn', are now the most planted. They form very hardy thickets that are often impatient to bloom when the autumn arrives, some upright posies of white and pink opening before the leaves have all been shed. But they will rarely be out of impressive bloom the first half of the winter. 'Dawn' follows the lead of its parent *V. farreri* in producing a series of upright stems and then softening this outline with many lesser ones arching outwards. The whole bush, up to 4 m (12 ft) high, can be covered with the scented, pink-budded, opened-white flowers for months. 'Deben' is whiter, and more rigidly upright. I grow an unnamed prolific clone that makes a bush much wider than tall, a pleasing rounded shape.

One other deciduous viburnum vies for top popularity. This is early summer-flowering *V. tomentosum*, which is distinctive with its series of horizontal branches built layer upon layer, the design emphasized in bloom when each spreading branch is lined its length with flat white clusters of flowers, like some surrealistic waiter balancing plates on arms. Each flowering package of tiny fertile flowers is generously encircled by large sterile ones up to 4 cm (1½ in) across. There are one or two well-known named clones such as 'Mariesii' and 'Lanarth' in which the horizontal design is particularly prominent and flowers are larger, up to 5 cm (2 in) across.

Evergreen viburnums have a special place. The Victorian favourite, *V. tinus*, is a very dense rich green foliaged shrub that can be left to form a thick rounded cloud shape but will respond to the knife and, whilst not being the leading topiary subject, can be kept in a more formal shape without looking hopelessly out of character. So well-known, it might get overlooked if we were not so grateful for the winter-long succession of blossom, wide posies of white scented flowers flushed pink in bud. 'Eve Price' is usually thought the best cultivar at present.

Most gardens if left to nature would soon become a tangled mass of scrub, so that it would seem that we are following a natural course if the main emphasis in our planted plot is on shrubs. This does not mean that all else is excluded, but it may well mean that the garden is given good shape, is always of interest and allows other plants, especially bulbs and ground cover herbaceous ones, to play a full role. This may well be the natural garden that you are looking for, one that looks well at all times, may take the minimum of tedious up-keep but can give enough challenge in designing, in planting new things and pleasant light maintenance.

CHAPTER 5

BULBOUS BONANZA

Many hardy bulbs can be planted and then left to grow for decades. Nothing gives such a feel of a natural setting as sweeps of bluebells or drifts of wild daffodils. One great advantage of these bulbs is that many produce colour and beauty well before shrubs and other plants, and then die away. If the right varieties are planted, they cause very little or no work and improve year by year. Bulbs planted and thereafter left alone are said to be naturalized.

NATURALIZING BULBS

There are two obvious places to plant bulbs in a natural manner: they look splendid between shrubs or in grass. However, it is a mistake to plant any bulbs in grass which you intend to keep carefully mown. First, they look like interlopers and, secondly, they cause a nuisance as one tries to manoeuvre the grass cutter around. Planted in rougher grass, this can be cut together with the bulbs' dying leaves six weeks after flowering, which is another reason for picking early-blooming bulbs. This six-week period usually means that the machine may be taken over the grass in late spring, before the garden generally takes on the look of a jungle.

PLANTING

Apart from choosing the wrong cultivars, the commonest mistake in naturalizing bulbs such as daffodils is to plant them too shallowly. As a rough guide, the amount of soil over the top of bulbs should be 10 cm (4 in) for daffodils and tulips, 8 cm (3 in) for *Hyacinthoides non-scripta* (bluebells), 5–8 cm (2–3 in) for smaller scillas, snowdrops, crocuses and most small bulbs. Anemones may be happy with just 2.5–5 cm (1–2 in) over their tops (Fig. 14).

Daffodils are the most widely planted naturalized bulbs. If these are planted too shallowly, the bulbs divide into many small pieces which produce plenty of leaf but little or no flower.

All bulbs are best planted in clumps or drifts to give a natural appearance. Any cultivation or weeding that needs to be done is easier if the bulbs are kept in definite plantings. Scattered bulbs are awkward and look very ineffective.

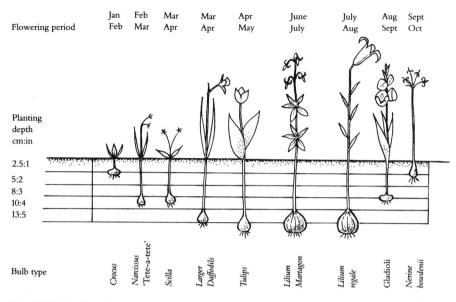

Fig 14 Bulb Planting.

CHOICE OF BULBS

There are huge numbers of different bulbs and the recommendations here are very selective, including only some of the most worthwhile kinds.

Snowdrops

Galanthus nivalis (common snowdrop) is as good as any of the rarer kinds, growing easily and increasing steadily. Whilst dry bulbs can be purchased and planted in the autumn, they do not particularly like being out of the soil for a long time and you can get better initial results from bulbs planted 'in the green' (whilst they still have green leaves). If you know someone who is willing to let you have bulbs, the very best time to lift them is when the leaves are just going brown. Then they should be planted immediately in groups but with a few centimetres or so between each bulb; they will soon grow into a thick clump. The double form, *G. nivalis* 'Flore Pleno', tends to open a day or two earlier but the many-petticoated flowers lose something of the chaste form of the single.

There are large snowdrop hybrids and forms. Good ones include *G.* × *atkinsii* and *G.* × *plicatus*. Avoid *G. elwesii*, as it sometimes does well and looks impressive, but then often fades away.

Crocuses

Also very early, at the end of the winter. For naturalizing *C. tommasinianus* is one of the most enchanting. There are several named cultivars but, if you can get seed, this grows quickly to flowering size corms and you may get a selection of colours ranging from the more or less standard pale mauvey blue to dark purples and other thin candles of subtle pinky or blue greys, and some white. Sown between shrubs, the seedlings will produce grass-like leaves and then be flowering in a couple more years. Just a little more fat and happy is *C. chrysanthus*, a species with very floriferous corms. Its basic colours are white, cream, yellow, bronze, blue, and mauve, but the outside of the buds are usually intricately marked with dark scroll work. There are no poor forms.

Narcissi (daffodils)

The names daffodil and narcissus are interchangeable, they mean exactly the same thing, the first is the common and the second the botanical name. Daffodils lead the spring bulb offensive against the winter. Many of the early-flowering kinds are excellent for planting and leaving to grow naturally. The wild English daffodil is *N. pseudonarcissus*, a species widespread in Europe. It is a protected plant in Britain, but one or two bulb dealers have supplies. At 20–24 cm (8–9 in), it looks just right in grass with its pale cream and primrose trumpet flowers. Bulbs may take a year to settle, after which they will increase steadily by bulb division and, given time, by seed. *N. obvallaris* (Tenby daffodil) is the same height but has uniform bright golden flowers with broad petals and stouter trumpets. It flourishes between shrubs and in grass. Both plants obligingly die down early so that grass can be mown.

Some of the very best naturalizing daffodils are the hybrids of the little species *N. cyclamineus*. The best known of these is 'February Gold' with longish crowns and petals tilted slightly backwards. It is a tough bulb that increases quickly. 'Charity May' is a softer yellow with wide petals swept backwards and a large bell-shaped flanged crown. 'Jack Snipe' has recurving white-pointed petals and small golden crowns. One of the most lovely is 'Jenny' which stands about 25 cm (10 in) high, with lots of flowers that open white and pale primrose but become all white after a few days. It looks very graceful, with long petals gently reflexed in a sweeping arc to point upwards, whilst the chaste narrow trumpet looks down. The persistence of the flowers is one of the many useful attributes of all these hybrids. Their swept-back petals gives them an informal and slightly wild look which, together with their relatively modest size, makes them ideal for naturalizing.

Earliest of all the cyclamineus are 'Tête à Tête' and 'Jumblie', which may have one, two or even three flowers to a stem. The bulbs increase rapidly and the smaller bulbs produce stems with only one flower, but this does not really matter as they are produced in such abundance and last so long – up to eight weeks!

'Tête à Tête' opens with golden flowers on stems about 10 cm (4 in) long, but these increase in length as the flowers age. 'Jumblie' has rather longer trumpet-crowns and the petals reflex more. They will do well between shrubs, mixed attractively with heathers, around the base of a specimen tree and even in grass.

The larger and more brilliant of the modern hybrids do not really look at ease naturalized. But there are some larger kinds than those recommended above that do grow well left to themselves in grass or elsewhere. 'Brunswick' is a tall kind with triangular white petals and a bold crown painted tones of shining pale lemon. Another good cultivar is the very old 'Van Sion', the early double yellow which sometimes has the doubling restricted to inside the trumpet but usually bursts through this restriction to make a full blown double, in form an imitation of a rather informal paeony. It has been grown in our gardens since the beginning of the 1600s, and seems to settle down happily wherever it is put.

Tulips

These are not normally thought of as naturalizing bulbs, as most of them look too formal and brilliantly dressed. However there are a few species that may be planted and left for ever to grow without attention. These are best in warm well-drained soils, perhaps in a rock garden or between small shrubs. *Tulipa turkestanica* is a small-flowered species with flowers open in late winter or very early spring. Each stem produces several, widely spaced blooms of small white stars with golden centres. In mid- or late spring *T. tarda* produces a clutch of green buds in the centre of a starfish rosette of flat green leaves. The buds open as stemless, quite large white and golden stars. Like the rather similar all-yellow *T. urumiensis*, it increases well in warm spots.

Some of the popular early-flowering *T. kaufmanniana* hybrids will persist and grow in numbers in well-drained soil provided they are free of slugs. It is certainly worth trying some; we have clumps that have been undisturbed for six years and look better each spring.

Bluebells

Bluebells, whether they are our native *Hyacinthoides non-scripta* with narrow flowers and curved stems, or the Spanish bluebell, *H. hispanica*, with upright stems and wide open bells, must be planted with some foresight. In most soils they can begin to increase at a rate that is alarming where you want them to behave with decorum. Where you want to establish wide stretches between shrubs, under trees, or in grass, the more seed they drop and bulbs they produce the better pleased you will be.

OTHER SMALL BULBS

Many of the early, small bulbous plants look natural by shrubs and produce colour when the shrubs are asleep. Winter aconites can be planted 'in the green' in the same manner as snowdrops. Their bright yellow buttercup flowers in the early weeks of the year are very welcome. Chionodoxas, *Scilla sibirica*, puschkinias and anemones like to be left alone and produce plenty of bloom in the spring. The anemones are really not true bulbs but are rhizomes treated in the same way. *A. nemorosa* is the wild wood anemone and a very pretty wildling. *A. apennina* and *A. blanda* are Europeans that grow easily, being plants of similar size but with many-petalled flowers of varying colours, including very attractive blues, pinks and whites.

SUMMER LILIES

As spring moves towards summer, some of the larger bulbs come into their own. Lilies are magnificent, although the more brilliant hybrids can be a little too showy for the natural garden and may need more attention than some of the others. The first to open is likely to be *Lilium pyrenaicum*, with its yellow flowers of curled up thick petals dotted black. This is followed by *L. martagon*, which at 1.2–1.8 m (4–6 ft), is twice as high. The standard kind produces narrow pyramids of hanging flowers with petals curled back into cylinders. Their colour is a pinky mauve, but there are deep maroon and pure white forms. Both species can be planted and left for a lifetime or two. They bloom from early summer for several weeks.

Other lilies that can be planted and left include some of the N. American species like *L. pardalinum* and the form *L.p. giganteum*. These bloom in mid-summer with large hanging flowers, the recurved petals being golden orange towards the centre and vermilion at the tips, and heavily spotted to give it the common name of leopard lily. These bulbs will be planted 10–12 cm (4–5 in) deep in the soil and will then increase well year by year. None of these will object to lime and all will grow in most soils, including heavy clay. They are at their best when grown as bold clumps between shrubs. They like to have their roots kept cool but to have their heads in the sun.

AUTUMN BULBS

The autumn can be a time when it is difficult to find fresh flowers apart from the michaelmas daisies, chrysanthemums and dahlias. But there are some bulbs that perform well late in the year, the most dramatic being the South African *Nerine bowdenii*, the only species of its genus that is hardy in cool climates. Suddenly in the autumn flower spikes pierce through the soil and arise 30–40 cm (12–15 in) without any accompanying leaves. A rounded bunch of bright pink flowers opens and lasts for weeks in prime condition. This is an unusual bulb in that it does not like to be deeply planted, so the long-necked bulbs should be planted with their tips just under the soil surface. Leaves appear after flowering in the winter or spring and then die away by the end of the summer. A warm well-drained spot should be chosen and then, although they may be slow in their first year, they will come each following autumn and increase in a very satisfying manner. Nerines resent disturbance, so once planted leave them alone. Even when crowded they will continue to flourish and only when they are very thick indeed, perhaps after eight or ten years, should they be lifted, split up and replanted.

Colchicums, often still wrongly called autumn crocuses, have many forms that bloom in the autumn with flowers that look like large crocuses. *Colchicum autumnale* is pinky mauve with some chequered markings. More showy is the species *C. speciosum* with large globes of rosy mauve. The white form is particularly splendid. They are sometimes called 'naked ladies' as they appear without any leaves. However, a word of warning: these leaves are massive when they appear in the spring, many from a corm and up to 30 cm (12 in) long and 5–8 cm (2–3 in) wide. You should plan for them; perhaps the corms should be planted between shrubs where the leaves can be somewhat lost.

True autumn-flowering crocuses are usually rich violet or mauvey purple shades, though there are also white forms. One of the best species is *Crocus speciosus*, with large globe buds that open to show orange stigmas in the centre. In well-drained soil it can start seeding, so that with corm increase it becomes pleasantly numerous.

CHAPTER 6

MEADOW AND GRASSLAND

A good lawn looks well, but also very artificial. If there is room enough in the garden plot and you are willing to spend time on keeping a lawn well groomed, then it can 'set off' the rest of the garden. In a sense it becomes the frame to the picture. However it is expensive both in terms of hours of labour and of machinery, and it is difficult to justify its place in a very small garden. The need for space to walk and sit can be met by paved areas, by the use of gravel, brick, wood or shredded bark. The patio, a type of outside room, is usually an integral part of garden design, and the obvious meeting place of house and garden.

An area of three or four square metres/yards up to something more expansive devoted to a 'natural' meadow/pasture can be very attractive, and most effective if it is also well defined either as a formal oblong shape or with an ungeometrical outline. If a part of the lawn is to be converted into a wild grassland area this can be marked simply by maintaining a precisely mown margin. Even if the whole lawn is converted, the edges could be kept neatly mown both for aesthetic reasons and the practical one of making at least a partial barrier for the seed of wild plants that are welcome one side but on the other could be annoying weeds in cultivated areas. In a large-scale grass wild garden, a curving mown path through will make the whole area accessible, even after rain. Alternative margins could be made of paved paths, gravelled areas, or low walls of brick or stone.

Meadows that are mown, or pastures that are grazed, really maintain an artificial balance of plants by periodic cropping, which ensures that larger plants are kept in check and the space is not taken over by a succession of stronger colonizers ending with scrub and trees. The gardener will have to act the part of the farm mower or cropping animals. The difficulty will be to choose when to cut with scythe, strimmer, or grass cutter. Some sacrifice of later-blooming species might seem to be needed. This can be avoided by thoughtful planting. It makes good sense to group spring, summer and autumn plants separately so that certain areas can be cut with the minimum of loss. Many early flowers will produce a second crop after being mown.

MAKING A GRASSLAND GARDEN

The plan of action could be as follows.
1. Select an open area, preferably of not too rich soil. The vegetable garden

which has been enriched by cultivation and fertilizers is not ideal. We are not looking to have wild plants growing too lushly and out of character.

2. Eliminate all difficult perennial weeds, e.g. docks, thistles, nettles, ground elder, bindweed etc. Use a systemic weed killer such as Tumbleweed (glyphosate). If there are coarse and persistent grass species present such as couch-grass, these should be killed off.

3. In lawn areas remove the turf and stack to rot for use elsewhere. The removal of the top few centimetres/inches will help by taking away some of the most fertile soil, together with a good proportion of the dormant weed seed.

4. Dig over or cultivate soil and allow to settle. Rake and sow grass seed. Choose only fine grass species like *Festuca ovina* (sheep's fescue), the fine turf grass of the Downs, and *Festuca rubra* (red fescue). The important thing to remember is that you are not trying to produce a lawn and the usual recommendation of 70–100 g per sq m (2–3 oz per sq yd) can be drastically reduced to a scatter of around 20 g (½ oz), to be raked in lightly. This is best done in mid–spring or at the end of the summer.

There are many decorative small grasses that can be introduced for effect. I like the early-flowering tiny *Lazula campestris* (field woodrush), also known as Good Friday grass, as its 5–8 cm (2–3 in) high flowers are often open with developed anthers by Easter in its northern hemisphere home.

5. At the same time it is possible to sow directly wild flower seeds such as *Leucanthemum vulgare* (ox-eye daisy) (Fig. 15), *Lotus corniculatus* (bird's-foot trefoil), *Viola lutea* (mountain pansy), *Viola tricolor* (wild pansy), *Cardamine pratensis* (lady's smock), *Papaver rhoeas* (field poppy), *Thalictrum flavum* (meadow rue), *Galium vernum* (lady's bedstraw), *Campanula rotundifolia* (harebell), *Ajuga reptans* (bugle), *Euphrasia nemorosa* (eyebright), *Linaria vulgaris* (toadflax), *Primula veris* (cowslip) and others.

It is best to sow each species separately in two or three short straight lines, so that when each one germinates it is easier to distinguish the wanted seedlings from the naturally occurring ones.

6. Whilst packets of wild flower seeds may contain plenty, it makes sense to sow a small number in pots and treat them carefully, just as you would precious garden plants. Some rarer kinds might be exclusively raised this way, the seedlings being pricked out in pots and only planted out into the wild garden when well established. Any lack of spontaneity that initially might seem to suggest itself will soon disappear as the community of plants become established.

7. In autumn plant groups of bulbs such as the *Narcissus pseudonarcissus* (wild daffodil), *Hyacinthus non-scripta* (bluebell), and tuberous-rooted plants like *Anemone nemorosa* (wood anemone).

Fig. 15 Wild flowers: ladies' smock or cuckoo flower, wild pansy, harebell, field poppy and ox eye daisy.

8. Keep a check on unwanted plants such as groundsel, dandelions and others that might tend to seed themselves. Later it may be possible to allow a few dandelions, but the choice depends on you.

9. Mow in late autumn, leaving only those plants which have winter appeal. Some few clumps of particular grasses, rushes, sedges, and the skeletal remains of

Opposite:
A corner of the garden where wild flowers are allowed a look in. *Silene dioica* (red campion) is in the front with *Lotus corniculatus* (bird's-foot trefoil), *Ranunculus acris* (buttercup), *Bellis perennis* (daisy), *Leucanthemum vulgare* (ox-eye daisy) and others in the grass. A curved path of brick makes a good contrast of texture and colour without looking too starkly utilitarian.

some summer-flowering plants like cow parsley can look decorative for at least part of the winter.

Mowing in late winter or very early spring will collect up any untidy bits, clear any grasses etc. that were left over winter, and leave everything ready for the early spring flowers. It should be done before the bulbs have made growth that would be cut.

10. Spring-flowering plants can be mown back by the end of the spring unless they are being kept for seed. Bird's-foot trefoil, with its eggs-and-bacon flowers, and the little pansies, tend to bloom a little later and so their patches will be left for another month or two. Lady's bedstraw will be at its best in the second half of the summer. Patches can be cut back as the flowers fade.

The aim is not to get an immaculate lawn decorated with flowers, but to keep the overall growth under control and to encourage plants that have flowered to grow afresh, to be ready for next year or to produce a second crop of later blossom.

DRY SOILS

Many of the pretty flowers of both pasture and meadowland manage well in fairly dry conditions. Those listed in no. 5 above will be perfectly all right. Among other wild flowers, you might try to include the following:

Anthyllis vulneraria (kidney vetch) is a scrambling plant with attractive pea foliage with the lead-leaflet much the largest and tight bunches of golden or orangey pea flowers with green bracts below. Flowers fade to tawny brown.

Centaurium erythraea (common centaury) is a very lovely plant, with stems varying from 5–30 cm (2–12 in) high depending on site, and bearing on its branched upright stems many five-petalled stars of richest pure pink.

Origanum vulgare (wild marjoram) stands 30–60 cm (12–24 in) high with crowded domed heads of little pink flowers held in purplish bracts.

Polygala vulgaris (milkwort) is a tiny plant growing only some 5–10 cm (2–4 in) tall with lots of dark blue flowers from late spring through summer.

Thymus praecox (thyme) is a creeping plant with pale purple-pink blossom any time from late spring till late summer.

Veronica officinalis (heath speedwell) is perhaps the prettiest of the speedwells with creeping stems and relatively long spikes of lavender blue flowers reaching up 12–30 cm (5–12 in).

WETTER SOILS

Caltha palustris (marsh-marigold) is a bold, lush-looking plant with more or less rounded, broad, glossy leaves and plenty of brilliant golden blossoms (much larger than the largest buttercup) borne in mid- to late spring.

Cardamine pratensis (lady's smock) is the pretty mauve or white flower that opens from mid-spring to early summer in moist fields or ditches. It is sometimes called the cuckoo flower, its timing coinciding with the said bird's more vocal times.

Filipendula ulmaria (meadowsweet), common in damp ditches, has attractive pinnate foliage, with each leaf of perhaps nine leaflets, and flower stems reaching 60 cm–1.2 m (2–4 ft) and topped with small creamy white flowers gathered in rather informal wide plumes during summer.

Fritillaria meleagris (snake's head fritillary) is a native of Britain and Northern Europe, much prized by gardeners. Narrow leaves and stems arise from the fat white bulbs to open large square-shouldered hanging flowers of mauve, marked in a chequer-board fashion. Flowers appear in mid- to late spring. There are various colour forms including contrasting white ones. 20–25 cm (8–10 in).

Geranium pratense (meadow crane's-bill) grows in dryish places as well as moister areas, where it is more luxuriant. It has typical much-divided geranium leaves, and large flowers of purple-blue appearing in mid-summer to early autumn.

Hypericum tetrapterum (Square-stemmed St John's-wort) is a very upright sub-shrubby plant some 40–75 cm (15–30 in) high with simple oval leaves and crowded heads of small golden flowers any time from early summer well into the autumn.

Lychnis flos–cuculi (ragged robin) is the distinctive bright pink flower with deeply divided pointed flowers held on slender branched stems 30–75 cm (12–30 in) high from late spring into the summer.

Veronica beccabunga (brooklime), in contrast to *V. officinalis* (see page 62), grows in moist soil, in mud, or reaches into water. Stems and leaves are fleshier than other speedwells. The shining plants are well decorated any time from late spring till autumn with pointed spikes of bright blue open flowers arising from leaf axils.

ACID SOILS

Calluna vulgaris (heather) is a very widespread plant in the wild. Nurserymen grow many forms, some pink-red like the standard plant; others darker, larger, or white. Different cultivars vary in height from 15–60 cm (6–24 in). There are forms with golden foliage and some that are gold and flame coloured. The plants are of course shrubs that will stand proud of the grass through the winter. Older plants can be trimmed back if they get too tall.

Jasione montana (sheep's bit) has tight heads of small blue flowers from late spring till late summer on stems 12–50 cm (5–20 in) tall. It looks rather like a scabious but is no relation.

Potentilla erecta (tormentil) has buttercup yellow, four-petalled open flowers from late spring till well into the autumn on stems that may be from 5–50 cm (2–20 in) high. Basal leaves are rather like small strawberries; those on the stem are narrower and more lobed.

Potentilla palustris (marsh cinquefoil) grows in wetter areas to a height of some 15–45 cm (6–18 in), with pointed chocolate-coloured flowers from mid-spring to mid-summer.

Viola riviniana (common dog violet) is the blue-violet, unscented flower that can be found in woods, hedgerows and heaths, as well as in grass.

ALKALINE SOILS

Anchusa arvensis (bugloss) is a member of the forget-me-not family but covered with bristly hairs on leaves, stems, and flower buds. When the buds open at the top of the 15–40 cm (6–15 in) stems, the relationship to forget-me-nots is more obvious; vivid sky blue, five-petalled flowers stare unwinking any time from early summer till autumn.

Cichorium intybus (chicory) can be very spectacular from mid-summer well into the autumn. It stands anything from 40 cm (15 in) to a magnificent 1.2 m (4 ft) high, with a succession of wide, many-petalled daisy flowers in frank sky blue. It is an unusual autumn flower, which is more showy on bright mornings; later and in dull weather they tend to close.

Fragaria vesca (wild strawberry) is an amusing little plant to grow, with its pretty strawberry leaves of three leaflets, sprays of small white flowers and small sweet red berries.

Genista tinctoria (dyer's greenweed) is a small relative of the broom and can make a very useful brilliant golden focal point in the early summer but if cut back early it is at its best later, still in full bloom in the autumn. In the wild it can colonize stretches of poor common land or roadside verges. It makes a low sweep of green narrow branches curving up to a usual height of up to 30 cm (12 in) but it can double this. It has lots of crowded spikes of small pea flowers.

Helleborus foetidus (stinking hellebore) is a popular garden plant despite its unfortunate name. There is not usually any unpleasant smell associated with the plant unless flowers or leaves are crushed. It has dark green palm-like leaves and fountains of cup-shaped pale green flowers, tipped maroon from mid-winter till late spring. In the wild it grows in scrub or light woodland, but in the garden it will be happy almost anywhere and makes an impressive evergreen mound in the middle of grass. Lots of seed results in many babies around the mother plant.

Scabiosa columbaria (small scabious) and **Knautia arvensis** (field scabious) are pretty flowers from mid-summer till autumn and are useful in dry spots. Tight pin-cushion flowers on almost leafless stems are lilac coloured.

Vetches   There are many of these pretty pea-family plants. They appear mostly on neutral or alkaline grassland soils. *Hippocrepis comosa* (horseshoe vetch) can make wide circles of bright golden blossom any time from late spring till late summer. With pea-leaves having perhaps seven pairs of leaflets, it grows to about 10 cm (4 in) high but can lean against grasses or other plants to get up to about 40 cm (15 in). The bird's-foot trefoil is rather similar in growth but with less leaf, and flowers more often stained with orange. *Onobrychis viciifolia* (sainfoin) in purplish pink, *Astragalus glycyphyllos* (milk vetch) in cream, *Vicia cracca* (tufted vetch) with bluish-purple spikes, and the other vetches and their relatives are all attractive plants.

There are plenty of fine wild plants from which to choose. Of course, we must include *Primula vulgaris* (primrose). In damp places *Ajuga reptans* (bugle) can colonize wide areas with shiny vein-embossed leaves held close to the ground and spikes of purple-blue flowers in early and mid-summer. There are good dark maroon purple-leaved forms. In dry spots of broken soil the red field poppies also look very vivid.

It is a good idea to explore the local flora which may be expected to flourish in a wild garden but on no account should plants be dug up from the wild.

CHAPTER 7

WET AND WATERSIDE

WATER IN THE GARDEN

Having a pond or stream in the garden can add a magical element that transforms a pleasing garden into an outstanding one. On the other hand, a badly built or designed pond or stream will be a constant source of annoyance. In our natural garden any water needs to look an integral part of the scene, not a contrived experiment. A pool or pools with curved outlines and with one or two bold margin plants, such as irises, rushes or the like, will give the whole site a real sense of a complete living environment.

MOVING WATER

A fountain is out, as it is too artificial, but a small stream, perhaps falling over a rock or two to make a modest cascade of lively water, is certainly welcome. Falling water will absorb oxygen for plants, fish, and beneficial bacteria. The movement of water catching the light will bring to life the dullest scene. Even a short run of water, perhaps twisting a bit and ending in a small pool, will add immeasurably to the pleasure of the garden.

A small immersible pump can return water from the end pool to the higher head of the stream. The best effect will be obtained when the electricity to the pump is turned off and the stream becomes a series of narrow pools. In some gardens it may be possible to channel surplus surface water into the stream and allow for the excess to run away from the lowest point either into a bog garden area or into a drain. Most gardens are going to be without any natural surface water and here, once the pools forming the stream have been made, all that remains to be done is periodically to make up the water loss due to evaporation.

PLANNING PRINCIPLES

A series of pools can be made to resemble a stream. This will look natural if the head and apparent source of the stream is behind a largish rock or a shrub. Whilst the water is held by either prefabricated glass fibre units or the tough plastic butyl, the edges of pool or stream may be disguised by rocks or plants or both.

Too small a surface area of pond or stream is likely to be more bother than it is worth, not least because it is difficult to keep in an equable state that will suit plants, fish, and other animal life. For a pond, a minimum water surface area of approximately 2.5 sq m (25 sq ft) should be planned. Smaller areas are likely to heat up quickly, promote fast algae growth from spring onwards, and then in winter become frozen solid, thereby killing fish and other livestock.

A depth of at least 60 cm (2 ft) is needed for fish and for many water plants, including popular water lilies. Newts and dragonfly larvae manage with water depths of 5–25 cm (2–10 in).

WILDLIFE POND

A pond can be a teeming centre of life. Insects will abound. Birds will bathe and drink. Newts and frogs can utilize the facilities. A shallow-sloped entry will help smaller fry to get in and out of the water. Also some reeds, water iris, and assorted waterside plants will provide shelter and food sources for insects.

MAKING A POND

SITING
1. Choose an open site with full sun.
2. Avoid trees that not only block the sun but will drop leaves that will rot and poison the water.
3. Choose a position where you will get the most visual benefit, especially from the house or the patio.
4. Avoid the highest or lowest points of the garden. You may want part of the margin to merge into a bog garden, but even this area must have definite limits.
5. Site as near as practical to an electricity supply.

PREPARATION
1. Design pool shape, using a hosepipe or something similarly flexible to form the outline. Curves can be incorporated but will not then be too unnaturally sharp. Most pools will have at least two levels, the main deeper section around 60–75 cm (24–30 in) deep, the margins at least 22 cm (9 in) wide and 25 cm (10 in) deep (Fig. 16).

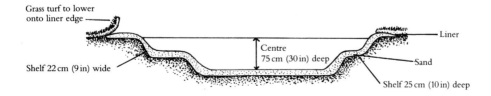

Grass turf to lower onto liner edge

Liner

Centre 75 cm (30 in) deep

Sand

Shelf 22 cm (9 in) wide

Shelf 25 cm (10 in) deep

Fig 16 Cross section of pool with liner or moulded form.

The magic of water and waterlilies and margin plants like the purple *Iris sibirica*.

2. Use pegs to mark the outline of the deeper part of the pool, and do the same for the outer limits. Remove the hosepipe.

If using a pre-moulded form, mark area needed and check levels of ground with spirit level. It is essential that the bottom of the excavation be level, so that the top of the mould is also level.

3. Tie string around pegs to give outline shapes.

4. Dig out soil from the centre deeper section. Often the soil is used to alter the contours of the ground close to the pool or stream.

If using a flexible liner, ensure that the bottom is as level and as free of projections as possible and arrange the sides to slope to help prevent soil slipping inwards.

5. Dig out the shallower margin area to a depth of 25 cm (10 in), and width at least 22 cm (9 in).

The whole of the pool may be so margined, or only such a length as you want to accommodate plants requiring this depth of water.

6. If a bog garden section is to be made this needs digging out to 45 cm (18 in) so that a polythene or butyl liner can be laid to provide a waterproof base.

LINERS

1. Remove turf or soil to a depth of 5–8 cm (2–3 in) and a width of 30 cm (12 in)

A rock garden made of slate, an unusual but effective treatment looking entirely natural and made more lively with the running water.

all round the excavation. This gives an area to tuck in the top of the liner under paving stones, rocks or soil.

2. The dimensions of liner required will be double the depth of the pool, added to both the full length and width. Better to err on the large than the small size.

3. Line the excavation with sand or moist fine soil to provide a snag-free base for the liner.

4. Lay liner across the pool and allow to sink in with an even overlap all round the margins.

5. Temporarily secure edges of liner with bricks, stones, or other weights. These may have to be eased up as the pool fills up.

6. The liner can be trimmed when the pool is full but 15–25 cm (6–10 in) extra is about right as the flap to tuck under the pool's edging of stones etc.

PRE-MOULDS

1. Cover the bottom of the excavation with 5–8 cm (2–3 in) of dry sand and lower in the pre-mould.

2. Check the pool bottom with a spirit-level to ensure that it is level along its length and width. Do this several times as work proceeds.

3. Down the sides, between the soil and the pool, pack dry sand for a quarter to a third its depth.

4. Gently allow water to fill pool to depth of sand outside and check that the pool has not gone out of alignment and is level. If all is not well, the water will have to be emptied and a fresh start made.
5. Continue adding sand around pool and allow water level to rise to same height until the pool is completely full.
6. Mask edges with stones, rocks and plants.

PLANTING

Some plants live their whole life in water, while others are to be found at the water's edge sometimes with their rootstocks under water, sometimes not. Still other plants enjoy the plentiful moisture of boggy ground but do not expect to be immersed. All these water-loving plants are well defined, distinct characters.

Water plants Underwater plants are important as they help to keep the water well oxygenated and to use the minerals that might otherwise encourage too much green algae. They can be introduced into the pool in plastic containers well tucked into heavy soil, with a thick top of gravel to stop the soil muddying the water. Usual plants available are *Lagarosiphon major* (common fish weed), *Elodea canadensis* (Canadian pondweed), *Ranunculus aquatilis* (water crowfoot) and *Hottonia palustris* (water violet). Canadian pondweed has a bad reputation for clogging up waterways, but it can be useful in a small pool so long as you keep an eye on its growth and remove any excess.

Water lilies help give the surface shade that is needed to create a healthy balance. There are tiny cultivars such as the white, golden, pink or red forms of *Nymphaea pygmaea* that will grow in water only 15–22 cm (6–9 in) deep. *N. × laydekeri* cultivars are rather larger flowered and need water just a little deeper. Popular *N. marliacea* forms in many colours are boldly flowered and grow in water 50–90 cm (20–36 in) deep.

Of the many other water plants *Orontium aquaticum* (golden club) is one of the most spectacular for spring and summer bloom. In deeper water the spear-shaped leaves float on the surface; in shallower water they tend to poke into the air some 30 cm (12 in) or so. White flower stems point upwards, their upper halves bright gold with a mass of tiny flowers that look as if the stems had been dipped in a paint pot.

Marginal plants There are some good plants that enjoy living at the water's brink. *Caltha palustris* (marsh-marigold) has lots of large lacquered buttercup blooms in spring, and the double form 'Flore Pleno' is even more impressive. The yellow flag iris, *Iris pseudacorus*, is a strong growing plant with impressive, upright, sword-like leaves and early summer flowers. It is too strong for the small pool. *Iris laevigata* from the Far East is a hardy deep blue-flowered iris that is a little less tall. *Iris kaempferi* has less foliage but magnificent wide-petalled blooms

Fig 17 Planting by the pool: 1. Iris. 2. *Caltha palustris* (marsh-marigold) 3. Large-leaved plant such as *Gunnera, Rheum palmatum* (decorative rhubarb) or *Rodgersia*. 4. *Astilbe*. 5. Rushes. 6. Waterlily. 7. Candelabra primulas. 8. Hostas. 9. Ferns e.g. *Osmunda regalis* (royal fern) or *Dryopteris dilatata*.

in many gorgeous colours (Fig. 17).

All the hostas do well in moist soils and can look very magnificent, with masses of plain or variegated leaves from spring till the frosts. Spikes of lavender or mauve flowers are a bonus.

Water-loving primulas such as *Primula florindae*, looking like gigantic cowslips, relish wet conditions. *P. japonica* is a leading water-loving species, a candelabra type with several spaced rings of flowers looking outwards. There is a wide range of colours, the rich coloured 'Miller's Crimson' and the contrasting 'Postford White' being two of the most effective and popular. They will reproduce themselves by seed, though individual plants will last several seasons. Other candelabra types include the rather daintier *P. pulverulenta* in its usual rich magenta colours and *P. bulleyana*, normally having salmon-coloured blossom on stems that, like the other species, can reach 60–90 cm (2–3 ft) high provided their roots are drinking deeply.

Very spectacular early in the year are the huge brilliant golden spathes of

A rock garden made of weathered limestone with a stream creating waterfalls. When the pump is turned off the water lies still in the series of pools. In the foreground *Juniperus* 'Pfitzeriana Aurea' is doing its best to look like a waterfall.

Lysichitum americanum. It should only be planted where there is plenty of room as the following leaves are large, at 30–75 cm (12–30 in) long. It is sometimes called the skunk cabbage – for its occasional evil scent – but this rather derogatory name really belongs to a relative, *Symplocarpus foetidus.*

More refined are the astilbes with their fern–like foliage and plumes of flowers in whites, creams, pinks and reds. The globe flowers, the *Trollius species* and hybrids, are pleasing with divided foliage and closed large buttercup flowers in various shades of yellow and gold. *Trollius europaeus* looks perfectly at home by a pool and has lots of limey yellow flowers that seem more natural than the somewhat glaringly extrovert colours of the *T. chinensis* hybrids.

One last suggestion is *Osmunda regalis* (the royal fern) that can grow into a most impressive plant with beautifully divided fronds reaching yards across. With winter the fronds die off but the rusty remains are still impressive.

CHAPTER 8

THE HERBACEOUS ROLE

The pure herbaceous border is an unnatural creation, nowadays rarely seen. Formal bedding is even more unnatural. However there are plenty of herbaceous plants that will grow in natural conditions and some that will even flourish in grass. Strong-growing plants like herbaceous paeonies will grow for decades in grass, gaining in strength rather than diminishing.

Most herbaceous plants find their garden home in beds and borders that contain shrubs and perhaps trees. These more permanent characters help to give shape and character to the plantings and will certainly be important in the winter months when the herbaceous plants die down to ground level. To save labour and for a more or less natural effect, shrubs may be planted fairly heavily and herbaceous plants used to give extra life, colour, and character at different times of the year.

In the natural garden it would be a mistake to use plants that need a lot of attention and that may need staking. Tall delphiniums will not do; the more usual hybrid roses are also not going to look right, although the shrubby kinds can be excellent; plants like many michaelmas daisies that require regular spraying and are better with support are not going to be right. However, we do not need to deny ourselves too many things as even michaelmas daisies can be represented by near relatives like the fine hybrid *Aster × frikartii* with wide-spaced flower heads of purple-violet for weeks in the late summer and autumn, a result achieved without any spraying for mildew and without constant annual lifting and splitting.

MIXED BEDS AND BORDERS

Obviously all gardening is a matter of unnatural contrivance. The mixed communities that can be housed in island beds surrounded by lawn or borders backed by hedges, walls, or fences are contrived but they can give a natural effect and the plants can grow in more or less self-perpetuating associations.

The following are some herbaceous plants that will look after themselves and will make good companions for shrubs and trees.

Acanthus
There are few more imposing foliage plants than the bear's breeches. Probably

the widest grown is *A. spinosus*, with dark green polished leaves much divided into sharply pointed segments. Plants steadily expand to form a mound of leaves at least 30 cm (12 in) long. Above this impressive looking spikey mass arise the 1–1.5 m (3–5 ft) strong upright spikes of curious hooded flowers in pale lilac, purple and green. Deep thick roots will persist for years to support the growing clumps. If you try to move the clump and bits of root are left behind they will produce fresh plants. This is a plant best given plenty of room to make an impact, it will do well in a groomed border but will hold its own against fierce opposition in a mixed wilder environment.

Alchemilla

There are several garden species but the much grown *A. mollis* (lady's mantle) is the one frequently used by flower arrangers during summer, when its 30 cm (12 in) high mound of round foliage is topped by a frothy mass of sulphur-coloured little flowers on intricately branched leafy stems. The foliage is a pale fresh green given a greyish cast by the slightly furry surface that helps each leaf to capture rainwater in its centre. It will increase by seeding itself, and looks pleasant either singly or in a group in an open sunny position. It will do well on very poor and dry soils as well as in more luxuriant quarters. If the first crop of flower is cut away, a lighter secondary crop is entirely likely.

Anemone

There are many kinds. Early in the year *A. nemorosa*, the wild wood anemone, is pretty in leaf and flower. There are pink and pale blue forms as well as the standard white with pink blush. Similar in habit and size are the many-petalled *A. blanda* and *A. apennina*. There are good rich blue forms of both, but *A. blanda* is particularly variable with various blues, white, pink, violet and red forms flowering from late winter to mid-spring. Height is just 10–13 cm (4–5 in) but they can be encouraged to colonize the front of a bed and between shrubs.

A. × *hybrida* is the name for the plants formerly known as *A. japonica*. These are tough persistent perennials that will last many decades as they advance their territory year by year. They are at their best in late summer and autumn, with many large white, mauvey pink or rosy flowers, single or double, and standing 75 cm–1 m (2½–3 ft) high. New plants will be a little slow the first year, as they resent disturbance.

Aster

The hybrid *A.* × *frikartii* has already been mentioned. It has an open branching form 75 cm–1 m (2½–3 ft) high, with lavender blue flowers from mid-summer till the frosts.

A. amellus 'Violet Queen' makes a neat plant that covers itself with richly coloured flowers in the autumn, some 40 cm (16 in) high. It is not prone to mildew.

Astilbe

With attractive, divided foliage, these plants like a moist spot and then produce plumes of flowers from early summer onwards, in pink, red or cream. 25–40 cm.

Dicentra

These look exotic and tender but grow well given a reasonable soil. The most popular is *D. spectabilis*, known by several common names including bleeding-heart and lady-in-the-bath. Succulent early growth unfurls beautiful ferny foliage, followed by leaning stems hung with cerise pink and white flowers. There is a pure white form. The whole is some 45–60 cm (18–24 in) high. *D. eximea* is much dwarfer with very divided ferny leaves and small bunches of flowers that can be rosy red, dull mauvey pink or white, according to variety.

Echinacea

The best purple cone flowers are those known as the Bressingham hybrids. They are strong plants with spear-shaped leaves and erect stems growing up to 60–90 cm (2–3 ft), with single, large daisy flowers of varying shades of rose- or salmon-purple petals pointing outwards from a dark central cone. There are white forms too that make a useful contrast. A group grown in the spaces between shrubs can be most effective for many weeks from mid-summer well into autumn.

Euphorbia

These are the spurges. *E. polychroma* makes a wide low mound of sulphur yellow early in spring. *E. griffithii* 'Fireglow' produces a number of erect stems from wandering underground shoots, with neat bronzed foliage and orange heads. *E. wulfenii* is evergreen in effect, with steel grey-green neat leaves and huge domed heads in shades of lime green. Standing 1 m (3 ft) or so, it can have a commanding presence for weeks through the spring. It produces occasional seedlings to increase its command of the garden.

Geranium

The true geraniums range from small alpine plants to vigorous plants 60 cm (2 ft) high or more. *G. sanguineum* (bloody crane's-bill) is a strong plant with attractive, divided foliage and magenta flowers from early summer to early autumn. Plants look well in borders, between shrubs or in grass. The most popular type is *G.s. lancastriense* which is a bright pink. Other large-spreading kinds are blue *G. grandiflorum* and rich puce *G. macrorrhizum*. With rather small leaves is the robust *G. endressii*, with mounds of well divided foliage and lots of rosy pink round flowers.

Opposite: Herbaceous plants that look after themselves, the geranium 'Johnson's Blue' is backed by the grey-leaved *Lychnis coronaria* and foxgloves, both of which regenerate with an abundance of seedlings.

Helleborus

Once planted these plants will continue to grow and bloom for decades. Boldly toothed foliage of *H. argutifolius* (syn. *H. corsicus*), gives a fine evergreen effect augmented in the first three months of the year with large bunches of apple green bowl-shaped flowers. *H. foetidus* is also evergreen, with narrow, dark green, palm-like leaves. It too blooms for months at the beginning of the year with fountains of goblet-shaped light green flowers lightly edged maroon.

The hybrid kinds of *H. orientalis* are exciting, with flower colours ranging from nearly black through all sorts of purples to maroon, mauve, pink and white. They may be uniformly coloured or decorated with lots of dark dots. They bloom through the spring, the plants resenting disturbance and being excellent between shrubs.

Hosta

These have been mentioned in the earlier chapter on water-loving plants (see page 71), but these magnificent foliage plants do well in most reasonable garden soils. A whole range of new hybrids is now being introduced, many from America. They range from very small-leaved plants like plantains, to magnificently large, wide-leaved opulent kinds in all shades from lemon to blue-green, some of the most effective being boldly variegated and with two or more colour shades on the blades of the broad-curved leaves.

Iris

Some of the best looking irises are those grown near water (see page 70). There are several variegated forms that do well in drier soils. *I. pallida variegata* is a form of the soft blue flowered June iris with wide fans of leaves; in the variegated form each leaf has a broad creamy white stripe down one side making a very decorative light effect. *I. foetidissima* 'Variegata' is a useful plant for shade with a strong tuft of shining leaves of dark green quite vividly streaked with bright primrose yellow. Small purplish flowers in early summer are insignificant, although they may be followed by the seedpods that burst open to show brilliant scarlet seeds. *I. pseudacorus*, whose variegated form is very effective in spring and early summer, has strong upright, sword-like leaves of green brightened with light golden stripes. The colour becomes more uniform green after mid-summer, and it produces the usual yellow flag iris flowers from early summer onwards. Whilst found wild in very wet places, in the garden it manages in most spots and can look impressive towards the front of a border as a punctuation plant.

Kniphofia

Red hot pokers can be red, yellow, cream, white or a mixture of these colours. The range of size is from a diminutive 15 cm (6 in) or so, to a towering 2 m (6–7 ft). They are at their best when left alone in a soil that does not get too dried out. The largest kinds are best at a little distance on their own and often towards the centre of an island bed or the back or a border. Especially in wetter districts, old dead leaves are pulled away in the winter and the clumps tidied up to some extent to prevent the beginning of any rotting in the clump's centre.

Ligularia

These are at their best in a deep moist soil, but we have managed on a thin soil over rock. Admittedly in times of drought they tend to flag and need a soaking before perking up. There are two very impressive kinds that are well worth a place where you need something bold and arresting. *L. dentata* 'Desdemona' has bold, rounded dark purple leaves and strong erect spikes up to 90 cm–1.2 m (3–4 ft) with narrow-petalled distinctive tangerine daisies at their best in the mid-summer months. *L. przewalskii* 'The Rocket', is a fine foliage plant with purple-black leaf and flower stems and wide rounded leaves that have dramatically toothed margins. The purple of the stems suffuses the leaves. Narrow long pointed spikes can reach 1.5 m (5 ft). Small, slightly dishevelled, daisy flowers make a rich golden contrast above the mound of foliage. The flowering display is at its best in late summer, but the plant takes on a distinctive role from the time it starts to grow in the spring. If you can find a moist spot it will look splendidly healthy and manage to combine a naturalness with a theatrical presence. It is trouble-free.

Paeonia

Cultivars of these strong plants will last even in rough grass left untended for many years. What paeonies like is a deep soil and an open airy spot. Usual colours are pink, red and white, but there are yellows. Whilst the large double ones like the pink 'Sarah Bernhardt' are very popular, the singles like the anemone-centred 'Bowl of Beauty' with wide pink flowers and golden stamens may be thought even more beautiful by some.

Polygonum

Some polygonums are weeds, like knotweed and black bindweed. Others are useful vigorous plants such as *P. bistorta* 'Superbum' (snakeweed), which grows quickly in moist spots with dock-like leaves and many upright wiry stems with pink poker or bottle-brush flowers. 'Donald Lowndes' is a low mat-forming plant for the front of the border or on the bolder rock garden. This cultivar produces lots of dense spikes of pinky red through the summer and into the autumn. It can be useful groundcover between shrubs.

Rodgersia

There are one or two species sending up large leaves like those of a horse-chestnut, but from strong rhizomes growing over or just under the soil surface. They enjoy moisture and, depending on the supply they get, will grow 40–75 cm (15–30 in) tall. The flowers are loose plumes of pinky red.

Ligularia przewalskii 'The Rocket' with yellow spikes and handsome foliage. In front is red *Lychnis coronaria* and blue *Nepeta* 'Souvenir d'André Chaudron', a very superior catmint!

Rudbeckia

There are several late-blooming perennial rudbeckias that can be very decorative for weeks through the autumn. One of the finest is 'Goldsturm' which has relatively small pointed oval basal leaves lost under a mass of flowering stems from mid-summer through possibly four months, with a 1 m (3 ft) mound of deep golden daisies with dark brown cone centres. The huge number of flowers in long succession makes this plant worth installing in borders and between shrubs although it will be best divided after three years and the youngest of the older portions moved to fresh sites. This is one of very few herbaceous plants listed in this chapter that need this treatment, but it is such a generous and useful plant that this small periodical service is a small price to pay.

Sedum

There are many sedums, some frankly weedy, but the well known ice plant, *Sedum spectabile*, is an easy large plant with an almost architectural presence, having whorls of thick succulent grey-green leaves and wide, almost flat, plates of autumn flower heads that attract the late butterflies. I have counted over two dozen drinking from a single clump. The distinctive, richly rust-coloured flower heads can be left through the winter. It is a plant which does well in poor soils and in dry awkward spots, always provided is is open to the sun.

CHAPTER 9

LAST LOOK ROUND

PLANNING FOR YEAR ROUND APPEAL

A garden that is only colourful and interesting for some weeks in the spring and again in the summer is really a poor thing. After all the winter is our longest season, often stretching over five months! We certainly need to limit its reign by planting things that will look well late in the year, and to have lots of very early spring bulbs as well as strategically placed winter-flowering shrubs, trees and plants. If winter is well planned for, the other seasons almost look after themselves.

WINTER – THE ROLE OF EVERGREENS

The real winter season begins with the dropping of the deciduous leaves and the dying back of herbaceous plants. It is then that evergreen plants take on almost sole responsibility for keeping the garden from looking a forlorn empty stage. The range of colours and forms of evergreens can be lively. A mass of dark conifers could be funereal, but blue-green *Chamaecyparis lawsoniana* 'Pembury Blue' can contrast with the golden effect of *C.l.* 'Lane' or the smaller slow-growing erect yellow yew, *Taxus baccata* 'Standishii'. Low-growing junipers come in many colours, from yellow through many greens, to almost blue. One of the most deservedly popular kinds is *Juniperus* 'Pfitzeriana Aurea' with wide-reaching, lemon, sweeping branches with slightly pendulous habit so that whilst eventually covering several square yards, it will only grow a very few feet high.

Whilst first evergreen thoughts may be of conifers, there is plenty of other choice. The heathers make an interesting pattern of foliage colours through the winter, the rather dark standard green being augmented by many brighter ones, some pure gold, others lemon. Some *Calluna vulgaris* forms are vividly painted with orange. Of course the *Erica carnea* types will have much of their foliage covered with long-lasting blossom through the winter months. They can take a leading role from autumn till spring in providing frost-proof bright colours. There should be no need to create just a uniform low carpet, the different cultivars vary a little in height and, by planting rather taller ones such as *E.c.* 'King George' on somewhat higher ground, and low ones such as dark-leaved *E.c.* 'Vivelii' in lower spots, the natural contours can be exaggerated.

A sweep of heathers in a position where they will be easily seen through the winter will bring them repeated praise in these months. They are also tidy the rest of the year. Further variety can be added by planting one or two of the tree heathers, such as *E. arborea*, that will slowly build up in soils not heavily limy to impressive plants some 1.5 m (5 ft) tall, although in favourable areas they can more than double this. *E.a. alpina* is more likely to be content with a 1.25–1.5 m (4–5 ft) maximum height, and can be pruned back if it seems to be getting too tall. There are white and pink forms.

A few dwarf conifers will look well with the heathers. *Thuja orientalis* 'Rheingold' is one of the most popular and useful. It makes a rounded pyramid-shaped bush that is slow growing to reach head height eventually, but only after many years. It looks bright in golden tones through the growing months and in winter takes on an attractive warmer cast, a rusty orange shading. It contrasts in form with the low heathers.

Variegated holly comes into its own in the winter. 'Golden King' and 'Silver Queen' are two popular dark-leaved kinds with very bold bright golden and cream-variegated margins. They are a little slow to grow at first, but then begin to accelerate and make a significant contribution to the garden scene.

Some of the other evergreens commonly seen can be overlooked just because they are so common; but the laurel and *Aucuba japonica*, cultivars often incorrectly known as 'spotted laurel', can both be worth a place in some garden designs. There are smaller leaved laurels that look neat, with slanting firm stems and quite showy sprays of white flowers. The aucubas are particularly useful in difficult dry, shaded corners where little else will grow. Those with plenty of gold on their leaves will help to give this type of awkward spot a bright, well furnished look. Do not despise golden privet; it will stay evergreen and bright in all but the most severe of winters. It is also a useful bush for cutting wands of foliage, to augment interior floral decorations.

Ivy, too, is something that can get overlooked, but there are literally hundreds of kinds to choose from. Many interestingly shaped and marked kinds take on pink, mauve, and purple tints in the winter. 'Buttercup' is one of the brightest of all, with traditionally shaped leaves in very bright yellow shades.

Whilst some silver-leaved plants can get slightly weary and worn looking in the wet of winter, this does not apply to the silver-leaved eucalypts. *Eucalyptus gunnii* is the kind that is often coppiced every other spring to keep it as a bush of rounded juvenile leaves. It does tend to reach for the sky if allowed its head, but if you want a mature tree with long flat pointed adult leaves, it may be a good plan to take a two or three year-old specimen and cut it down to a stump of a few centimetres/inches, selecting three or so of the resulting new shoots to form an interesting multi-stemmed specimen. *E. niphophila* is rather slower to scrape the heavens and has lovely silver-white bark and orangey young foliage. It too looks more interesting with several trunks, or as a fairly closely planted group.

THE ROLE OF THE DECIDUOUS

Deciduous trees and shrubs can play a part. The intricately twisting branches of the contorted willow *Salix matsudana* 'Tortuosa' can look even more interesting without leaves when the branches are silhouetted against the sky and every loop is decorated with hanging drops of rainwater. The silver birches show off their bark, the most dramatic being *Betula utilis* 'Jacquemontii', which makes a very evenly shaped tree that looks freshly painted 'brilliant white'. Dogwoods can glow with their brilliant young shoots. *Cornus alba* 'Sibirica' is the brightest red, but the ordinary *C. alba* is also attractive with rather more maroon-red stems. Dogwoods melt into the natural garden very easily in borders and grow especially well in moist spots. To get the best stem colours, bushes can be cut back almost to the ground at the end of the winter.

Alternative-coloured stemmed characters which are especially good in the winter include a number of willows that will be coppiced every other year to encourage fresh strong growth from ground level. From quite a number that can be treated this way, the following willows are particularly good and will grow in normal soil, though they will of course relish a moist spot. *Salix alba* 'Britzensis' is orange-red, *S.a.* 'Vitellina' is yellow, *S. daphnoides* is violet, usually with a very attractive white 'plum' bloom.

WINTER FLOWERS

Flowers are available in winter. Amongst the shrubs the witch hazel has to take pride of place. *Hamamelis mollis* is a spare-branched shrub that grows slowly but, from being a small specimen, it decorates each bare twig with brilliant golden flowers in the depth of winter and remains undamaged by frost. Petals are narrow strips; they look like miniature paper decorations. There are a large number of hybrids on offer now, some more orangey or tawny red, but few any brighter than the species. Provided you are not going to sell the house and garden next year, one of the witch hazels should be a top priority choice, one bright specimen in winter is worth half a forest of other things blooming in summer.

As a complete contrast, one could plant *Garrya elliptica*, a dark-foliaged evergreen that redeems any suggestion of gloominess with innumerable, very long tassel catkins of silver, olive and green through the winter months. Whilst it is often planted near a wall, it is perfectly all right in the open in any save the most exposed of cold areas.

Evergreen *Mahonia japonica*, or one of the hybrids such as 'Charity', has firm upright stems with classy evergreen leaves, rather like holly leaves which have

Opposite: Informal pathway through various plants including variegated hostas and ferns. Shredded bark is used as a weed-inhibiting mulch.

been ironed flat. They top each stem with several sprays of hanging cup-shaped flowers, lemon in colour and scent.

The well known evergreen *Viburnum tinus* is useful for its rounded cloud-shaped bush of rich dark foliage, very freely covered with wide posies of white and pink-scented flowers. The deciduous *V. farreri* has tight bunches of perfumed white flowers but pink in bud. The species has been put into the shade by the even more free-flowering hybrid 'Dawn', which can start flowering with the end of the autumn and be decorative for months. Even an initially small specimen will be making a very worthwhile contribution in two or three years. Thereafter it will be so free flowering that it will be a natural target for flower arrangers wanting some sweet-scented blossom for either small table decorations or to augment larger ones, which may be predominantly coloured bark and foliage but need the added liveliness of blossom.

The winter-flowering cherry *Prunus subhirtella* 'Autumnalis' makes a spreading, medium-sized tree that starts blooming in the autumn and is scarcely ever without lots of small white or light blush flowers through the winter, though it may pause in prolonged, very frosty weather. For winter effect it is difficult to think of a more useful and modestly proportioned tree.

One of the most exciting plants in the middle of winter is the Algerian iris, *I. unguicularis* (*I. stylosa*), which can be planted at the base of a house wall or in similar difficult spots, where its fare may be frugal but it is likely to get well warmed through the summer. Amongst the tuft of narrow leaves appears a winter succession of quite large flowers, velvety in texture and usually a brilliant violet-mauve but with intricate veining and flashes of gold. Buds or flowers can be plucked and brought inside to enjoy all the better. Established plants provide many scores of such blossoms.

BULBS

Bulbs can certainly help to brighten the winter. Snowdrops will grow naturalized in grass, between shrubs and in many odd corners that are transformed by their presence. Once planted they can be left for ever, but if you want to increase them and the clumps have got fairly crowded, the best time to do this is some six weeks or so after flowering when the leaves are becoming less lively but the clumps can still be easily seen and lifted. The bulbs can be teased apart and replanted immediately, best in groups with an inch between bulbs. Bulbs increase most quickly in an open cultivated soil full of humus. In such positions not only do the bulbs split but they will send out stems at the end of which new bulbs grow.

Crocuses can be helpful. The late autumn species will continue into the beginning of winter and then, before spring arrives, the earliest of the new year kinds will start opening. The species look more natural than the fat Dutch hybrids. *C. chrysanthus* forms in white, yellow, blue, and other shades are good in front of beds and between shrubs. These species can be grown in light grass but are rather less successful in heavy grass and certainly not where the grass is meticulously mown. In strong grass one may have to resort to the larger Dutch hybrids which will persist for years if the grass and their leaves are not mown too early. (By late spring it should be safe to take the machine over the grass.)

Of the species *C. tommasinianus* is the most inveterate colonizer where there is open soil. It produces slender pointed buds in shades of lilac and lavender which open to stars in sunshine. Fat seed pods follow, freely produced and held close to the ground. The resulting seedlings grow to flowering-size corms in two or three sessions if not hoed out. The leaves can look a little like grass when young.

Daffodils belong to spring but some are very early and intrude into the winter. The little 'Tête à Tête' and 'Jumblie' will be in evidence before spring really arrives. Both start flowering with one, two or three shining gold blooms to 10 cm (4 in) stems that lengthen to double this as they age. They can be left down for several years before getting so crowded that they need lifting and splitting.

LOW MAINTENANCE

GRASS
Natural gardening will often mean less work than the usual regime, but no gardening is effortless. For the maximum effect with the least work, heavy reliance will be placed on shrubs and trees. Grass as lawn or natural meadow has to be tended. If a meadow is attempted, broad pathways running through will need to be regularly cut. With lawns, a good groomed green effect can be achieved without bringing the cutters as low to the ground as if trying to make a bowling green. An extra couple of centimetres of grass growth will keep it looking greener in times of drought and is easier to keep attractive than a very close trim.

MULCHES
All cultivated areas where grass is not allowed can be kept weed free very much easier if well mulched. These mulches perform various functions: apart from smothering weed they keep the soil temperatures and moisture contents more equable; they tend to encourage a better soil structure as organic materials rot to add to the humus content of the soil.

In rock gardens or beds the mulch may be of rock chippings or pea gravel. It is surprising just how efficient a layer of such inert material is in conserving moisture. Rock garden plants also enjoy the instant drainage away from their low leafy parts and some insulation of soil temperatures is also provided. And of course it looks a tidy and attractive background for the plants.

In other places mulches are likely to be made of shredded bark, compost or peat. Well made and fully rotted compost is excellent as it improves the soil structure significantly and provides food from the time of its application.

Shredded bark may well be the most useful for low maintenance. If bought in large quantities it is far less expensive than purchased bag by bag from the local store. The bark looks attractive and, if spread as a generous 8–10 cm (3–4 in) layer over the soil around plants and shrubs, it will defeat all but the most persistent weeds. It makes sense not to mulch before ensuring that weeds such as bindweed, couch grass, docks and nettles are eliminated. A very great advantage of shredded bark is that it is slow to rot, so it will usually be an effective mulch for at least three seasons. It may divert some of the population of soil bacteria towards this rotting operation, bacteria that would otherwise be producing nitrogen for plants. Therefore it makes sense to accompany a mulch with a dusting of fertilizer, either nitrogenous like sulphate of ammonia, or a general one like Growmore that contains nitrogen but also provides phosphorus and potash.

Peat has been the gardener's standby for so long that it comes as a shock to many to realize how its use has resulted in the destruction of the natural ecology of different parts of the world. The use of coconut fibre and shredded bark has the very great benefit of being a renewable resource that could otherwise be treated as a waste product. The cost of using peat as a mulch can militate against it, and it is not as practical as either compost or bark, as once dried out it forms a surface almost impervious to water. Alternatives to peat are now being marketed; these are often mixes of several forms of organic matter. They can be used in composts or as mulches, and are often far more effective than peat.

MAKING COMPOST

Much has been written about this in the past, and really every garden should have some arrangements for making compost, even if only on a modest scale. To burn leaves, as some gardeners still do in the autumn, is a sacrilegious act. Most organic matter can be reduced quite easily to a crumbly humus that is pleasant to handle and is the lifeblood of the soil.

On the smallest scale, leaves and other similar forms of organic matter can be composted by being gathered up and placed in a closed plastic bag such as a bin liner. To get as thorough and quick reduction of the material into compost, it will help to mix the ingredients completely with a thin scatter of soil and to make sure that all is slightly moist but not soaking wet. A light dusting of sulphate of ammnonia will be helpful by providing nitrogen to aid the bacterially organized rotting. If the mix is placed in a bag and left sealed, but with air inside, the material will rot in good time, quicker in the months when the temperatures are higher than in the colder winter.

Efficient rotting will depend on several factors: the quality of the organic material, the presence of the appropriate bacteria, moisture content, adequate air, and the ambient temperature.

Material that will rot easily includes non-woody garden weeds and rubbish, kitchen food waste such as potato peelings, paper, natural fibre clothing and other materials, grass cuttings and straw. Hedge clippings with a high proportion of woody tissue can be composted but will take longer to reduce to crumbly humus; the same may be said of materials such as leather waste and sawdust.

To make the material easily available to the bacteria, it helps if it can be reduced to a more or less even mix, meaning that no one item is dumped in large quantities without admixture onto the compost heap. If considerable quantities of compost are going to be made, it may be worth considering investing in a shredder. A shredder is a most useful tool for converting piles of intractible-looking waste into a manageable-looking product. Most will deal adequately with woody prunings up to perhaps 4 cm (over 1 in) thick, the resulting shredded chippings being perfectly all right to incorporate in the bulk of composting material.

Whilst initially these machines may appear to be expensive to buy, they are durable and can help to provide quantities of valuable compost quicker and more efficiently. Choice of machine will be governed by two main factors, their efficiency and their safety. Like all machines with moving parts, and in this case, sharp blades, they are potentially dangerous. Ones to avoid are those where it is possible to insert a hand to the blades whilst they are moving. But certainly shredders make the job of composting a pleasure rather than pure toil.

COMPOST BINS

Choice of size of bin will obviously depend on the size of the garden and the enthusiasm of the compost maker. A small garden is likely to have an intermittent supply of rubbish for composting. Keen composters will grab the opportunity to augment their supplies at times like the autumn when there can be a glut of fallen leaves. At other times it may take months to fill up a bin not much bigger than the average dustbin. Of course where there is a reasonably sized lawn there can be a lot of grass clippings when the lawn is growing strongly. Bins work most efficiently when they can be filled in one go with a mixture of produce. A mass of grass clippings will need leavening with other material. Little more than a 15–20 cm (6–8 in) level of clippings should be entered before alternating with a layer of some such material as loose horse manure, or rougher garden rubbish with a scatter of soil. Grass clippings by themselves will tend to form either a water-resistant thatch or to become a slimy mass that on drying sets solid as concrete.

The best manufactured bins for the average suburban garden will have a capacity of something approaching 1 cubic metre (36 cu ft). However if supplies of compostable produce are limited, then a smaller bin of not less than .25 cu m

(9 cu ft) should be adequate and one can expect to fill this in 4–6 months. Unexpected gluts of material can be kept in sealed black plastic sacks until there is room in the bin to accommodate them.

Within reason, the larger the container the more even the rotting and more uniform the resulting compost; material at the edges is less likely to remain dry and unrotted.

Rotting compost needs air and water for the bacteria and fungi to work efficiently. Too much is as bad as too little. This means that the bin needs a lid and that the sides are best solid, with some airholes rather than just wire-mesh.

Where lots of compost is to be made, a permanent structure can be built with four upright posts and strong boards, such as old floor boards, nailed round the sides. Dimensions of such a bin are not critical but could be approximately $2 \times 1.2 \times 1m$ ($6 \times 4 \times 3ft$). One side is arranged so loose boards can easily be slotted in and out. This makes it easier to load and unload the heap. Two bins, or a double one, is the ideal; whilst one is approaching maturity the other can be loaded with fresh produce.

The complete compost should be a crumbly, almost black material without traces of material not decomposed. It will be invaluable for making up soil mixes for potting, for enriching soil prior to planting, or as a mulch.

TOOLS

Most expensive is the tool or tools to cut grass, that is mowing machines and strimmers. In very small gardens it may be best to forgo the lawn and have any open area paved or gravelled. With the margins sympathetically treated by allowing the encroachment of creeping plants, the paving or gravel need not destroy a natural appearance.

In such very small gardens, if no wide open area is planned, vistas may be maintained by planting low-growing plants like heathers, and natural pathways can be made through these by the use of shredded bark. Stepping stones may be incorporated if they are securely laid and, by their nature do not stay wet and become slippery. Wooden 'stepping stones' can sometimes be faulted because they become covered with a hazardous layer of algae or moss.

A few good quality basic tools would include a spade, fork, rake, hand trowel and pair of secateurs. A sheet of plastic or a manufactured weed-tidy is useful for removing garden rubbish to the compost heap or incinerator/bonfire site/garbage bin. The remaining tools that may be considered are a flat hoe and a sprayer. A hoe run through the top 2–3 cm (1 in) of soil quickly defeats germinating weed seed and helps create a loose layer of soil that acts partially as a mulch to protect the soil below from excessive moisture loss.

A strong plastic sprayer holding some 2.5 l (½ gal) of liquid can be used against weeds, fungus afflictions and pests. Full-time chemical warfare is not recommended; however early applications against greenfly, other pests, fungus diseases and weeds will save much labour later on, and it can be done without hopelessly damaging the environment. A squirt in time can save ninety-nine! Some gardeners keep two sprayers so that one can be clearly marked as the weed-killing instrument, whilst the other is used exclusively for insect and fungus disease treatments, as well as for the application of foliar feeds. If only one sprayer is used it needs to be washed out especially well after every sortie.

WILD LIFE

There has been much written recently about the encouragement of wild life. Gardens are the homes of many birds and insects. Most gardeners have always encouraged birds, save perhaps the fruit-bud-eating bullfinches and such marauding pirates as the magpies. Insects are now more often than not seen as beneficial and are allowed to maintain their place in the overall population, but action will be organized against such successful creatures as the cabbage-white butterflies when they invade foodcrops, nasturtiums and other plants.

NECTAR AND POLLEN FOR INSECTS

Cotoneaster horizontalis and other species become alive with bees when in flower. Berries are eaten by birds in the autumn/winter.

Viburnum tinus and other species, *Mahonia* and *Chaenomeles* forms provide early sustenance for insects.

Brooms and rose species are enjoyed by bees. Heathers and thymes are also much visited.

BUTTERFLY PLANTS

Buddlejas and michaelmas daisies are favourite butterfly flowers. *Sedum spectabile* is the leading member of a genus attractive to butterflies, with plenty of nectar late in summer and autumn. *Centaurea* (knapweed) and *Tanacetum vulgare* (tansy) are welcome stand-bys.

WILD LIFE

The garden pool is a very lively centre for plants, insects, birds and other forms of animal life, and can become almost the heart of the natural garden scene. Make sure that one side at least has a shallow entry point where frogs and other animals can get in and out easily. Clumps of iris or similar plants will make the water more accessible to birds and other creatures; many need some cover to approach with confidence.

Excessive tidiness is not going to help wild life. The birds will enjoy turning over fallen leaves to find their food below; a fallen rotten bough can become a tenement for all sorts of small creatures; and a corner where a pile of dryish natural material lies can become the over-winter quarters for a hedgehog. Seed heads of many plants provide food for finches and other birds. Shrubs that produce edible berries look marvellous in fruit. Most of us do not begrudge the birds their share.

ACKNOWLEDGEMENTS

The publishers are grateful to the author for kindly granting permission for the reproduction of all the colour photographs in the book.

All the line drawings were drawn by Nils Solberg.

INDEX